JUMP COURSE

DESIGN MANUAL

JUMP COURSE
DESIGN MANUAL

How to Plan and Set Practice Courses
for Schooling Hunter, Jumper, and Equitation Riders

Susan D. Tinder

Foreword by Micca Henry-Sowder & Randy Henry

TRAFALGAR SQUARE
North Pomfret, Vermont

First published in 2012 by
Trafalgar Square Books
North Pomfret, Vermont 05053

Printed in China

Warning and Disclaimer of Liability
Riding and handling of horses is a hazardous activity, which can result in injury or death. The author and publisher shall have neither liability nor responsibility to any person or entity with respect to any loss or damage caused or alleged to be caused directly or indirectly by the information contained in this book. While the book is as accurate as the author can make it, there may be errors, omissions, and inaccuracies. This book provides general information, instructions, and techniques that may not be suitable for everyone. No warranty is given regarding the suitability of this information, the instructions given, and/or the techniques described herein. Qualified personal instruction is suggested to best understand the ideas presented in this book.

Trafalgar Square Books encourages the use of approved safety helmets in all equestrian sports.

Library of Congress Cataloging-in-Publication Data
Tinder, Susan D.
  Jump course design manual : how to plan and set practice courses for schooling hunter, jumper, and equitation riders / Susan D. Tinder.
     p. cm.
  Includes bibliographical references and index.
  ISBN 978-1-57076-560-5
 1. Equestrian centers--Design and construction. 2. Architecture and recreation. I. Title.
  SF294.5.T56 2012
  725'.88--dc23
                         2012027594

All photographs and diagrams by Susan D. Tinder unless otherwise noted.
Book design by Lauryl Eddlemon
Cover design by RM Didier
Typefaces: Open Sans, Officina Sans

10 9 8 7 6 5 4 3 2 1

Contents

Foreword

by Micca Henry-Sowder and Randy Henry

"What do I do with that pile of jumps?"

This is a question anyone who has ever set a course has asked him or herself. As trainers, we have experienced this dilemma *many* times over the years, often using valuable lesson time to build courses for our students to school.

We have our own facility, as well as teaching at other locations, including Sue Tinder's farm Tolland Falls. Sue took it upon herself to start setting some jumps, then courses, before her own lessons, so we could spend more time teaching (and she and her horses could spend more time learning) and less time building courses. This book is based on her experience and what she's learned through years of training and showing over fences, hours of study, and the kind of trial and error we all experience when setting fences.

The *Jump Course Design Manual* is an informative and easy-to-use guide to help you get started designing and building your own jump courses. Sue takes a whole lot of guesswork out for you, providing instruction in course design, choosing course components, and setting courses with safe and accurate distances for different disciplines and ability levels.

And always remember: jumps move, so don't be afraid to move them. Go ahead and make these exercises and courses your own.

Micca Henry-Sowder and Randy Henry
Winsome Farms, Denver, Colorado

Micca Henry-Sowder grew up in the hunter/jumper industry. She is a second-generation trainer and equestrian facility owner. Her students have gone from short stirrup to indoors to Grand Prix.

Randy Henry has nearly six decades of experience and is repeatedly hired by world class riders and trainers for consultation and coaching. She actively mentors young professionals seeking help and advice to navigate through a most difficult equestrian career. Randy is a big "R" judge and past USHJA committee member.

Preface

This book is the resource that I wish I had when I first started to design and set courses at my farm, Tolland Falls Equestrian Center, in Sedalia, Colorado. Even though I have shown on the AA-rated hunter/jumper circuit for almost 15 years, I had never really paid attention to what it took to build an actual course. I needed a resource that discussed how to build courses and explained the principles behind what the rider needs for schooling at home. I wasn't trying to build a Grand Prix jumper course or design courses for a horse show, but I wanted more than the usual suggestions for gymnastic lines and grids that are included in most instructional books on jumping.

When I decided to set my own schooling courses at home, I discovered many things "I didn't know that I didn't know." I was faced with such questions as: Where do I buy jump components? What jump components do I need to buy, and what sizes? How do I store and maintain them? I also knew that I wanted my own courses for schooling, but designing and setting a course that made sense seemed daunting.

In the beginning, I used to set a course by standing in the middle of the ring with a jumble of standards and a pile of poles. I would throw out a few poles and move them around until I had something I thought would work.

Oftentimes there was one particular exercise I wanted to incorporate; I'd start by setting up that exercise and then try to work the rest of the course around it. Usually, after most of the course was built, I would realize that I no longer had a good track to the exercise I wanted to work on, or perhaps some other element was now in the way. So I would start moving things to create the track I needed and end up setting the course multiple times before I finally finished.

It didn't take long for me to realize how hard moving jumps around an arena was for one person to do on her own! I decided I should research and educate myself on a better way to design and set the courses I needed to school. I wanted diagrams to use as a communication tool so that I could enlist helpers when possible. I needed to know—*before* I started taking components out to the arena—*what* I was going to build the fences with and *where* I was going to place the fences in the space available. I also wanted to keep the arena neat and uncluttered, and I wanted to make sure that the courses I set would allow the footing to be maintained and worked, which is one of my facility's biggest investments.

I learned course design principals with the help of qualified professional instruction, through reading, and

via my own personal observation of how the course diagrams at horse shows translate into riding a "good round." I have gained experience through plain old hard work and dragging jump components around an arena. I didn't learn any of what I now know overnight, and in truth, I learned how *not* to set a course long before I became capable of doing it well.

Within this guide, I share the principals of course design in layman's terms and offer course diagrams taken, or adapted from, my own course library. These courses are reflective of my personal training program and may not be appropriate for all riders or all training programs. However, it is my hope that they can provide information and inspiration as you begin to design courses that will meet your own objectives.

I have included a significant number of photographs that illustrate the jump construction that is used at horse shows, as well as examples of specific obstacles that I have used at my farm to give you ideas of what you might want to build or buy. Note that in these pages I don't suggest how to *ride* these courses, nor do I specifically state what kind of questions each course is asking; rather, I simply offer suggestions for appropriate types of "furniture" and where they are best placed in your "riding room."

I have found that studying course design has been one more step in my journey toward improving my understanding of the technicalities of jumping, and therefore, my riding and success in the show ring. My goal is to be safe, challenged, and to feel a sense of accomplishment from my riding. Most of all, I want to continue learning about the sport I love. I hope that you find this guide useful, and I wish you a safe and satisfying experience as you progress toward your own riding goals.

Susan D. Tinder
Sedalia, Colorado

Acknowledgements

Special thanks to Micca Henry of Winsome Farms, my trainer, whose skill, enthusiasm, and encouragement make riding a lifelong learning experience.

For their constructive criticism and review of the material, I would like to thank: Julie Bachman, Kelly Boyd, Tracy Corwin, Cynda Dyer, and Liza Dennehy.

Thanks to Eliza McGraw for her encouragement in launching this project and for her introduction to the wonderful people at Trafalgar Square Books: Rebecca Didier, Martha Cook, and Caroline Robbins.

And finally a big thank-you to Ivan and Armando for providing the help to gather, set, and move the jumps for the courses I set at home, as well as the courses you see in this book.

1

INTRODUCTION TO MODERN JUMP COURSE ELEMENTS

- **Arena Footing: Type and Management**
- **Anatomy of a Jump**
- **Structural Elements and the Horse's Perspective**
- **Fence Types**
- **Jump Course Basic Terminology**

PHOTO COURTESY JAMEE HAINES

Not so long ago, horse show jumping courses were set up in a field or over open terrain. The jumps consisted of post and rails and occasionally a gate, coop, or a natural bank jump. The tracks for the courses themselves were simple and often only had one lead change. There were fewer divisions and the fences were set much higher than they are today. Measuring for a distance was almost unheard of. The course designer was usually the person who owned a few jumps and had a truck to transport them to a horse show!

As the industry became more safety-conscious, and as our understanding of how the horse sees and perceives his surroundings and obstacles before him improved, course design evolved. Along with other safety rules, there is now a mandate for wearing approved safety helmets, using only safety (breakaway) jump cups, and ensuring safe and proper footing in horse show arenas. Most recently, the United States Equestrian Federation (USEF) has passed a ruling that only licensed course designers may be used for rated competitions. The licensing process is rigorous and can take several years to complete.

⋀ Horse show photographs are often taken from the *back side* of the fence with the horse jumping toward the camera—as shown here—which makes it hard to tell what the fence actually looks like. Throughout this book, I have tried to include as many pictures as possible with the jumps depicted from the front side of the obstacle in order to illustrate how a typical jump is constructed. In this picture you can see the *front side* of some of the other jumps included in this course.

PHOTOS BY ROBERT K. TINDER, 1974

Ⓐ Not so long ago, horse show jumping courses were set up in a field or over open terrain. The jumps consisted of post and rails and occasionally a gate, coop, or a natural bank jump.

As I mentioned in my introduction, I am *not* a licensed course designer. My intention is not to set competition courses, but to help you construct safe courses for schooling at home and ultimately meeting your training objectives. I feel that this can be accomplished by first understanding some of the important elements of the modern jumping course, beginning with something I take very seriously at my farm: arena footing.

ARENA FOOTING: TYPE AND MANAGEMENT

As the horse moves across the ground, his joints absorb shock created from the impact, loading, and breakover phase of the horse's stride. There is also shear force on the soft tissues of the leg during the propulsion phase that occurs as the horse's leg swings forward and pushes off. The strength of these forces depends on the horse's weight, speed, and the course of the motion. The harder the ground, the more concussion the horse's body has to absorb. When the ground is too soft, soft tissues are strained as the horse attempts to stabilize his stride. "Good" footing must be able to both absorb shock *and* provide a reliable, solid platform, which isn't too soft or too slippery, from which to push off.

According to *Under Foot: The United States Dressage Federation Guide to Arena Construction, Maintenance and Repair,* the best arenas have three layers: a *sub-base*, a *base*, and finally the riding surface (the *footing*). The sub-base is the existing ground below the top soil, and this layer has to be properly graded for drainage before adding the next layer (the base—see more about this below). Optimal drainage is achieved with proper grading and no low or high spots. Water needs to flow *around* the arena.

When the arena is at the base of a hill, there should be swales or ditches on the uphill side of the arena to keep water from running onto the arena surface, and swales should be built all the way around the arena if there is a general need to handle excess runoff.

As mentioned, the second layer, which rests on top of the sub-base, forms the base of the arena. The base layer provides support for whatever footing material you choose to use. It has to be solid, non-slippery, and non-shifting. It should be practically impenetrable and is often made from crushed stone compacted nearly 100 percent. For jumping arenas the base layer should be between 6 and 12 inches deep.

The top and final layer is the riding surface—the footing material itself. Arena footing needs to provide traction as well as cushioning. It needs to be deep enough to protect the horse's legs from concussion but not so deep that it strains tendons—between 2 and 3 inches, depending upon the compaction quality of the material used. The horse's hooves should not sink into, or "punch through" to the base layer. The footing should handle moisture effectively and maintain its resiliency by absorbing and retaining some water, rather than letting it all run off.

Many people say that the best riding surface is grass. However, grass surfaces can get too hard if proper moisture is not maintained, they quickly show wear when there is a lot of traffic, and in the case of constant or heavy rain, grass arenas can quickly become mud pits. Sand is

Here you can see the early stages of the footing at Tolland Falls: angular sand on top of a deep base of decomposed granite. The footing was subsequently treated with a bonding agent and a geo-textile footing additive for moisture retention and to reduce the shear value of the sand. Note that when you have a limited budget the most important things are consistency of footing and good drainage.

Harrow Teeth – Used to refine and aerate the footing.

Roller – Pulverizes and then firms the footing. The roller works in conjunction with the harrow teeth.

Channel Blades – Used for leveling and spreading the footing.

Chisel Plows – Rips the soil to the desired depth aiding cutting and leveling.

Arenas require routine maintenance to address such footing issues as consistency, hardness, depth, shear value, dust control, and drainage. This is an arena *drag*—or *groomer* from DJ Reveal (www.reveal4-n-1.com). The drag is an important piece of equipment for keeping your arena footing in great shape.

A

B

C

In Photos A and B, you see routine maintenance of the arena footing at Tolland Falls: applying a bonding agent to the footing and dragging the arena. In Photo C the footing is hand-smoothed between rounds at a horse show, which is necessary after a number of horses have taken the same track and ruts and divots develop. It is a good idea to have a rake handy at your home arena—just be sure to store it safely when it is not in use.

the most commonly used footing material because it is fairly durable, but it can become dusty as it breaks down over time and with use. As sand particles break down the shear value of the sand increases, reducing traction. This is why sand is now often amended with rubber or textile fibers to help address the shear issues, increase moisture retention, and add cushion.

In addition to footing additives, chemical bonding agents are often applied to footing material. Bonding agents also help with moisture retention, reducing dust in the arena. Chemical bonding agents do deteriorate over time, depending upon weather and arena traffic, and require reapplication.

ANATOMY OF A JUMP

Before I begin to discuss how horses *see* jumps, as well as different *types* of jumps, let me quickly touch on some basic terminology that I'll use throughout this book:

• **Standards** (or in some cases **pillars**) provide the frame for the jump. Standards support the poles and/or gates that rest in *jump cups* (see photo on right). The height of the jump is typically adjustable via holes or a track in 2- to 3-inch increments, starting about 6 inches

from the ground. **Wing standards** generally have two sets of "feet" at their base with pickets, lattice panels, or painted insets between them. Wing standards are generally 2 to 3 feet wide and are around 5 to 6 feet in height. **Schooling standards** are made up of one post (usually 4 by 4 inches square and 5 feet high) set in a simple, stable base. Schooling standards are often used when space is limited and to support the back element(s) of a spread

V Here is an example of an oxer (part of an option fence—see p. 122 for more about option fences) with various elements labeled. All components, except for the varnished wood poles, are from Burlingham Sports (www.burlinghamsports.com).

Decoration secured to a schooling standard (with a small bungee cord) for stability from the wind.

Schooling Standards

Varnished Wood Poles

Wing Standard

Metal Jump Cups with Pins

Flower Boxes as a Ground Line

Boxwood Hedges "standing" filler. Boxes, Walls and Hurdles sit on the ground between the standards rather than hanging from jump cups.

> Here you can see samples of fillers and ground lines as commonly found in the hunter ring. Photo A is a vertical with natural branches used for a ground line, short flower boxes behind them, then slightly taller wood boxes as a back drop for the flowers, followed by a gate with two poles hanging from the jump cups. Photo B is an ascending oxer, again constructed as befits the hunter ring, with a similar ground line-flower box-gate arrangement. Notice that the *spread* between the two pairs of jump standards is fairly narrow for an oxer. This is probably to compensate for the additional width of the fill elements on the front side of the jump. Note: Because of the aggregate width of this jump, the trajectory the horse will take when jumping it will be similar to the trajectory of a triple bar (see more about this on p. 12). Also, in International Hunter Derby classes, the depth of a ground line cannot exceed 18 inches, and this one appears closer to 3 feet.

fence, such as an oxer or arrowhead, or a hogsback, fan jump, or triple bar.

• **Jump cups** are made of either metal or plastic and are secured via a pin (see below) in holes or on a track built

into the standard. The United States Equestrian Federation (USEF) and Fédération Equestre Internationale (FEI) require that safety cups be used at all sanctioned events. Safety cups allow a jump to fall easily from the standard when hit. Safety cups are relatively shallow or completely flat (see photos on p. 199). The **pin** that slides through the side of the jump cup and through the standard should be permanently attached to the jump cup with a metal chain or a short piece of rope to prevent loss.

• **Poles** are typically 10 to 12 feet in length and between 3.5 and 4 inches in diameter. "Skinny" jumps may use poles as narrow as 8 feet in a jumper class and as narrow 6 feet in an equitation class.

• **Ground lines** are added to the base of jumps to give them "dimension," making it easier for the horse to judge the right takeoff point. For schooling purposes at home, a ground line is usually a simple pole rolled out 6 to 12 inches from the base of the jump, but flower boxes, turf boxes, or branches may also be used for this purpose, particularly in hunter classes at horse shows. Equitation classes may or may not have ground lines in front of the fences, and generally jumper classes do

not use ground lines at all. A *false ground line* is created when the pole, flower box, or other fill element is placed *behind* the front vertical plane of the jump. False ground lines are illegal for horse show purposes. (I discuss false ground lines in more detail, and provide sample images, on p. 8.)

• **Fillers** consist of poles, planks, panels, gates, or a combination of elements that *hang* from the jump cups attached to a pair of standards, or they can be components such as walls, boxes, hurdles, rolltops, liverpools, and flower boxes that *sit on the ground* in front of, or between, the standards.

STRUCTURAL ELEMENTS AND THE HORSE'S PERSPECTIVE

In the pages ahead I will discuss different kinds of obstacles and the elements of which they are made. When selecting the structural elements that will make up a jump course—such as the standards, poles, ground lines, and fillers I just listed, for example—it is helpful if you understand a little about how the horse *sees* each jump and how he determines the height and width of the obstacle.

The horse's eyes are located on each side of his head (rather than in front, like ours). This enables him to experience a panoramic view, necessary for a prey animal's survival in the wild. However, he also has a blind spot directly behind him, directly in front of him, and directly below his nose.

This means that when jumping the horse loses sight of the fence just before he leaves the ground. The decision the horse makes on the height and width of an obstacle has to be made on the approach to the fence. The horse first determines the takeoff point and then determines the height. In other words, the horse evaluates the jump from the ground up. This is why you don't want to set fences with what is known as a *false ground line*—it is hard for the horse to judge the takeoff point accurately. As mentioned on p. 8, a false ground line is created *when the filler is set behind the front vertical plane of the jump*, or *when the front element is set higher than the back element*, such as in a descending oxer (an illegal fence for horse show purposes).

It is believed that horses are less able to judge the width/depth of a fence than they are able to judge an obstacle's height and that they tend to gauge the width of an obstacle by its general appearance. If the fence looks substantial, or if it has a lot of poles, it is likely that the horse will think it is wide or deep. (This perhaps explains why horses tend to knock down poles on spread fences that are airy.)

The horse needs to raise (objects in distance) or lower (objects nearby) his head to keep objects in focus. There is an area of the equine retina that runs horizontally from side to side called the *visual streak*. When a horse focuses

> Photos A and B are of a roll top fence and demonstrate the difference between a *false ground line* and a correctly set fence. In Photo A, note that the fill elements are placed *behind* the front vertical plane of the fence (behind the pole on the jump standards). Because a horse judges the takeoff point from the ground up, *before* he determines the height he will have to jump, a false ground line makes the takeoff point visually deceptive (farther away than it really is). In Photo B, the roll top fence is set correctly with the filler set in *front* of the poles and standards.

on an object that is viewed *within* the visual streak, the horse's vision is very good. However, if the object is outside the horse's visual streak, his vision is poor. The horse must raise, lower, or turn his head in order to keep objects within the visual streak and in sharp focus.

Remember that blind spot in front of his nose? As a horse moves toward an object he has to raise his head to keep the object within the visual streak. This is why it is important when riding to let the horse raise his head on the approach to a jump. By the time a horse is a couple strides away from a jump, he has already determined the takeoff point and can no longer see the point on the ground where he will start to jump; he is now judging the height of the obstacle. As he starts to take off, the fence has entered his blind spot and he can no longer see it, at which point he is jumping on trust and experience.

There is continuing debate as to the degree to which the horse is able to see color. It appears they can discriminate between colors, although not as specifically as humans. Therefore, the color of jump poles, standards, and other course elements is not as important as the *contrast* between colors. Striped poles seem to be easier for the horse to see than single-colored ones. When selecting colored elements, take the color of the background into consideration. For example, plain green poles in a green field, or natural wood poles in a sand arena, are more likely to blend into the background and be difficult for the horse to see.

> A visually deceptive fence like the fence in A—sometimes called a "joker" fence—uses one rustic or unpainted rail and two wings. The lack of filler makes it difficult for the horse to judge his proximity to the base of the fence, as well as the fence's height. This type of fence is illegal for horse show purposes. Photos B and C depict two alternative ways to set an "airy" vertical fence that are acceptable for use in competition.

V Photo A is a vertical fence as might be seen in the hunter ring, and Photo B is an example of a vertical from a jumper course. Fences used in hunter classes are meant to simulate the type of elements that would be seen, or jumped, when foxhunting. Years ago, hunter classes were jumped outside the ring over open terrain or across a big field. Today, hunter fences are constructed using simple, natural-looking, plainly colored components, generally including a lot of greenery and flowers. Jumper fences, on the other hand, are built using brightly colored fill elements and striped poles.

It is important to consider the horse's perception when constructing a jump course—keep his visual abilities and limitations in mind as you choose the types of obstacles to include, as well as the materials that make up those obstacles.

FENCE TYPES

VERTICALS
Vertical or *upright* fences consist of one pair of standards with poles and fillers in the *same vertical plane*. A vertical fence should encourage the horse to fold his legs evenly over the obstacle and cause the horse to make a steeper trajectory over it than he would over a spread fence, for example (see p. 11). The exception to this rule is seen in

the hunter ring, where both the vertical and oxer fences tend to be a little "rampy"—a single jump may have multiple elements used as a ground line and graduated degrees of filler (see photos on p. 6).

SPREADS
Spread fences consist of at least two pairs of standards. Schooling over spread fences helps a horse develop scope as the horse has to jump *wide* as well as *high*. Spread fences may have multiple fillers/poles on the front set of standards, but only one pole is used on the back and middle (when applicable) standards.

Oxers
This category includes the *ascending oxer* (top pole on

the front set of standards is lower than the top pole on the back set of standards), one of the easier fences for a horse to jump as the "ramped" rails mimic the natural trajectory of the jumping horse. Ascending oxers are the only type of oxer allowed in hunter classes.

The *square oxer* has the top pole on the front pair of standards set at the same height as the top pole on the back set of standards, making it slightly harder to clear

than the ascending oxer because it does not follow the horse's natural trajectory. When the fence's front poles are set higher on one side and lower on the other, and back poles are set in an opposite formation, forming an "X" so the center of the obstacle is the lowest, it is known as a *Swedish oxer*. There should not be more than an 18-inch difference between the higher and the lower side of each pole. When the lower side of the poles are set

V Photo A is an ascending oxer: a spread fence where the top back pole is higher than the top of the front vertical plane so that it follows the natural ascending arc of the horse's jump. Photo B is a square oxer: a spread fence with the top back pole placed at the same height as the top of the front vertical plane of the fence. The Swedish oxer in Photo C demonstrates how the poles are placed in an "X" configuration with the lowest point of the jump in the center. Finally, in Photo D you seen a descending oxer—a fence that is set so that the top back pole is placed lower than the top of the front vertical plane (the front vertical plane is marked by the yellow arrow). This kind of visually deceptive fence is not used in competition.

Ascending
Oxer
Side Profile

A

Square
Oxer
Side Profile

B

Swedish
Oxer
Side Profile

C

Descending
Oxer
Side Profile

D

V Photo A is a triple bar—a spread fence with three sets of jump standards and poles set to ascending heights. Photo B is a hogsback, which features three sets of jump standards like the triple bar, but the front and back top poles are set to the same height with the pole in the middle set higher. An arrowhead or corner fence, shown in Photo C, has two sets of standards. On one side the standards are close together, and on the other side, they are further apart, so the spread changes from narrow to wide. A fan jump as you see in Photo D features a single standard on one side and two or three standards on the other, with poles set in an ascending manner.

on the ground, the fence becomes a cross-rail (see p. 14). Square and Swedish oxers are only used in jumper and equitation classes—you won't see them in the hunter ring.

As discussed, the *descending oxer*—where the front elements are higher than the back elements—is illegal in competition because it is a visually deceptive fence for the horse.

Triple Bars, Hogsbacks, Arrow Fences, and Fan Jumps

In addition to oxers, there are several other kinds of spread fences. The *triple bar* consists of three sets of standards with the horizontal poles or planks set progressively higher from front to back. The fence should always be built so that the middle rail is at least 6 to 12 inches higher than the front rail, and the back rail is 3 to

6 inches higher than the middle rail. The triple bar is an easy jump for a horse because the "ramping" arc of the obstacle is close to the horse's natural trajectory.

A *hogsback* is a cross between a square oxer and a triple bar. There are three sets of standards (like a triple bar) and the front and back rails are set at the same height (like a square oxer), but both are set at a height that is lower than the top pole on the center set of standards. The construction of a hogsback forms an arc shape so it is the easiest type of fence for a horse to jump because its construction follows *both* the ascending and descending arc of the horse's trajectory.

An *arrowhead* fence (also referred to as a *corner* fence) is an oxer where the standards on one side of the obstacle are placed closer together than the standards on the other, so the spread changes, depending which side of the fence is jumped. A *fan* jump has a single standard on one side with two or three sets of standards on the other, and poles set at ascending heights. It is a cross between an arrowhead and an oxer or triple bar.

❯ Raised cavalletti are valuable for training purposes. Both the adjustable cavalletti stands (middle and right) and the longeing standards (foreground) are from Jumpvc (www.jumpvc.com).

⋀ Here canter poles are set up in a straightforward rhythm exercise. Note that this picture shows a major "no-no": When you do not have a gate or a pole resting in the jump cups, the jump cups should be *removed* from the standards as empty jump cups are a safety hazard.

Two versions of the most common training fence: the cross-rail. When you set a cross-rail you want to make sure that you set the lower end of each pole so it rests on the ground to the *inside* of the standards as shown in Photo B. This way if the poles are hit they fall to the inside of the jump rather than rolling outward where the horse might trip over them.

A

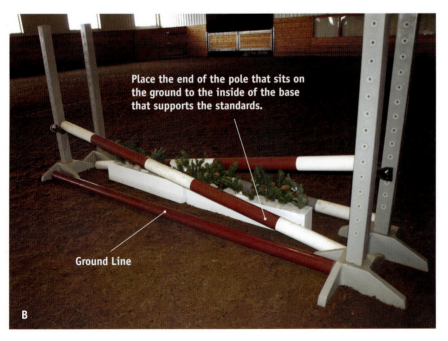

Place the end of the pole that sits on the ground to the inside of the base that supports the standards.

Ground Line

B

TRAINING FENCES

Ground poles are fence poles on the ground (trot or canter poles) and *cavalletti* are poles often raised just off the ground (set on blocks or short standards). Both are very useful, and quite common, for training purposes in a variety of equestrian dicsciplines. They help improve the horse's rhythm, stride length, and balance.

The *cross-rail* is a favorite training fence that encourages both horse and rider to jump straight over the middle of the obstacle—an important skill for negotiating any type of jump course. Crossed rails will help the horse and rider to see and maintain a track that causes the horse to travel directly over the middle of the fence and not jump to one side or the other, which is especially important when negotiating related elements such as lines and combinations. Neither cavalletti nor cross-rails are seen in the show ring.

JUMP COURSE BASIC TERMINOLOGY

A typical jumping course—whether in the hunter, jumper, or equitation ring—consists of seven to twelve jumping efforts (jumper courses have a minimum of ten). About half the fences in any given course will be verticals, and the remaining fences will be spreads. The lower the level of the class is, the fewer spread fences you will see. Horse show rules normally require that courses have at least one lead change. This is referred to as a *change of direc-*

tion and means that roughly half of the jumps are taken off the right lead and half are taken off the left lead.

A jumping course follows a predetermined *track* that is drawn out by the course designer. The track determines the order and direction that each jump is to be taken (see p. 16 for diagrams). In hunter classes, a flower box is typically set as a ground line on the front side of the fence, indicating direction. In jumper classes, colored flags on the jumps indicate direction: the red flag should be on the rider's right and the white flag should be on her left. A course may consist of *straight* tracks, *diagonal* tracks, *circular* tracks, and *angled* tracks.

• **Straight tracks** run parallel to the arena wall. Riders approach and/or clear the jump perpendicular to its center (90 degrees) and parallel to the sides of the arena.

• **Diagonal tracks** run at an angle to the arena walls and are typically (but not always) used to change direction and change lead. Riders approach and/or clear the jump perpendicular to its center, but on a track that is at an angle to/from the sides of the arena.

• **Circular tracks,** such as a rollback or a bending line (see p. 44), can also be used to cause a change

of direction; simple turns and corners while maintaining direction are (semi)circular.

• **Angled tracks** can be straight, diagonal, or circular, but indicate that the rider approaches and/or clears *the jump* at an angle that is either greater than, or less than, perpendicular to the obstacle's center.

Once the track has been established, jumps are placed upon it as a *single* jump, a *line* of jumps, or a *combination* of jumps.

• A **single jump** is a fence that is jumped by itself without any related distance to the next jump.

• A **line of jumps** consists of two or more fences that are related to each other through a specified distance *greater than three strides*. Lines can be *straight, diagonal, bending,*

Ⓥ Here you can see a basic course with a few of its elements labeled. Color-coordinating the fences in the lines (see the diagonal and outside lines) helps the rider memorize and navigate the course.

Single Oxer

Diagonal Line

Single Vertical

Outside Line

or *broken*, and they can be placed anywhere within the confines of the arena as long as there is adequate room for a safe approach and landing. A straight or diagonal line indicates the rider will jump the fences center to center on either a straight or diagonal track. The fences in a bending line are also jumped center to center, but the track has a curvature to it that allows the horse to stay on the same lead for the entire line. A broken line is also curved, but the arc of the track running to the succeeding jump is on the counter-lead.

• **Combinations** are two or more jumps that are related by *fewer than three strides*. A double combination has two related jumps and is sometimes referred to as an *in-and-out*. A triple combination has three related jumps that are set so that there are not more than three strides between any of the elements. It is not uncommon to have a line lead into, or out of, a combination.

V This simple course diagram illustrates some basic jumping course terminology.

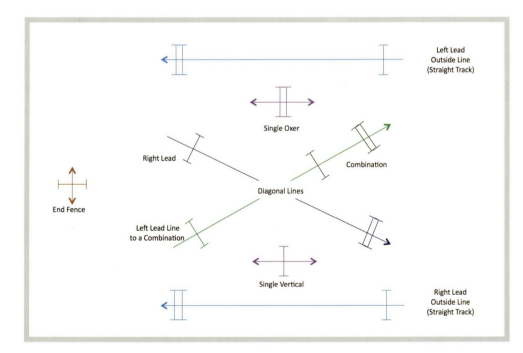

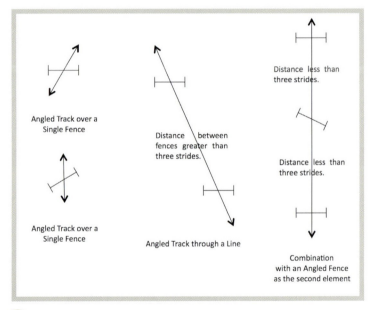

^ An angled track is not really a track but rather refers to the angle that a fence is to be jumped. It can be any fence that is to be jumped at an angle that is either less than or greater than perpendicular to its center (90 degrees). An angled track is a more advanced design element, as "seeing a distance" to jumping on an angle is much harder and requires a greater degree of control over the horse.

Combinations are two or more jumps that are related by fewer than three strides In Photo A you see a two-stride vertical to vertical combination (an in-and-out) in the hunter ring decorated with natural elements. Photo B shows a two-stride square oxer to vertical in-and-out" in the jumper ring (note the red and white directional flags and fence numbers).

HALF-TURNS AND HALF-TURNS IN REVERSE

When designing jump courses, you may employ a *half-turn* or *half-turn in reverse* to change direction. Most beginner and hunter-type courses use only half-turns through the corners or to change the direction of the track. When the change of direction is through a half-turn, the lead change happens after the jumping effort. A half-turn is fairly easy turn for the horse because the lead change starts during the suspension phase of the canter stride (or as the horse is in flight over the fence), and as a result, allows for the horse to more naturally change his lead and stay in balance upon landing. This results in a smoother, more flowing ride around the course.

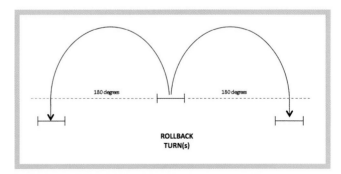

A rollback turn is an immediate turn upon landing from a jump with the track taking you in the opposite direction of travel. Usually the track is purposely set so that it is on a narrow arc when traveling to the subsequent fence. When setting rollback fences you need to make sure that (1) they are set at an angle to each other that is 180 degrees or greater, and (2) the distance of the arc for the rollback track is a minimum of 25 to 30 feet wide (at least three strides through the arc). You should also have enough room for at least two or three straight strides upon landing from the first fence prior to turning and two or three strides to get the horse straight to the second jump after making the turn.

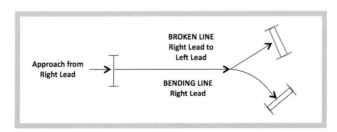

A bending line is jumped from the center of one fence to the center of the next, on a curved track that allows the horse to stay on the same lead through the entire line. A broken line's track requires the succeeding fence be jumped from the counter-lead. Fences used in bending and broken lines should generally be set at a minimum of six strides apart. This is especially important for a broken line where the horse needs to be straight for at least one stride in order to change leads before bending toward the second obstacle. The fewer strides between obstacles, the more technical these kinds of lines become.

In handy hunter, equitation, and jumper classes, a half-turn in reverse is often used somewhere on course, especially if the course takes an "S" type track. This turn is more technical because the lead change has to happen just before the rider switches the bend on the approach to the fence. The rider has to consciously ask for, and set the horse up properly, to make the lead change, requiring more finesse. The more room you can allow between fences that require a half-turn in reverse, the easier it is for the rider to keep the course smooth and flowing.

How It Works

When you perform a half-turn when riding on the flat (without fences), you turn away from the rail toward the center of the arena and circle back toward the rail while maintaining the bend—all in the same direction. You change to the alternate bend *after* you have made the half-turn, just before you return to the rail. Therefore, if you are cantering a half-turn, the lead change happens *after* you have completed the change of direction, at the point the horse's body is straight and just before you ask him to bend in the new direction on the rail.

The half-turn in reverse is a somewhat more difficult turn because you don't have the rail to help encourage the horse to change lead. When performing a half-turn in reverse, you come off of the rail, change your bend (and/or lead) and *then* turn back toward the rail to reverse direction. This means that when you are cantering a half-turn in reverse, you have to change your lead *before* you start to circle back in the opposite direction so that you are on the correct lead for the turn itself.

When performing a half-turn or half-turn in reverse on course between fences, the same pattern that you would use on the flat applies. It is important when designing courses to understand how the type of turn is influenced by the placement of the jumps so that a course rides smoothly.

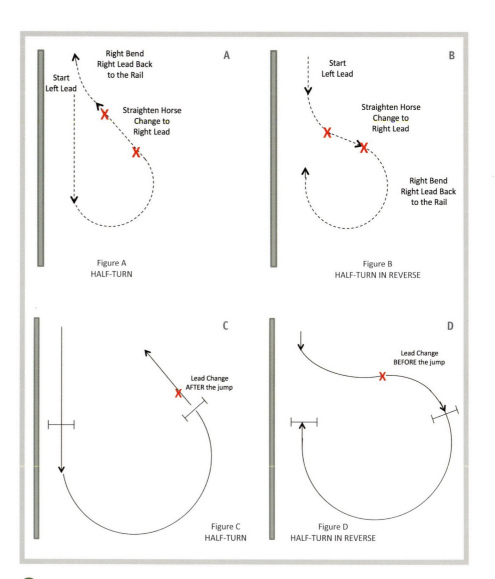

The half-turn and half-turn in reverse on the flat and on course.

2

DISTANCES

- **What Is an Appropriate Distance?**
- **Distance Ranges**
- **Takeoff and Landing Distances for Different Types of Fences**
- **Fence Type and the Horse's Forward Motion**

WHAT IS AN APPROPRIATE DISTANCE?

Learning how to determine and set the appropriate distance between related obstacles is one of the biggest challenges for any course designer. When designing courses at home, you should adjust the distances, as well as the jumps that you choose to use, to be appropriate for the horse and rider schooling them. But what does that mean, exactly?

In truth, there is no perfect set of distances that work in *every* situation for *every* horse. Yet in order to set exercises and courses safely, it is necessary to have an understanding of what is generally accepted as an appropriate distance for lines and combinations, and to know how to adjust those distances to fit your specific situation. It will help if you know how the term "distance" is actually used in the hunter/jumper world. It can be somewhat confusing, as the term can have different meanings when it comes to jumping an obstacle or when setting, or walking, a course.

"SEEING" THE DISTANCE

For riders, distance is the word they use to describe *the point where the horse leaves the ground when jumping a fence*. This takeoff spot is a direct result of the stride length, pace, and track that was created by the rider on the way to the jump. A horse can leave from a long,

Because learning to "see" a distance is one of the hardest skills for a rider to learn, setting correct distances for schooling at home is just as important as setting the distances correctly for a course at a show. This colorful in-and-out combination is from JUMP4JOY World Class Jumps (www.hitech-horsejumps.com). Notice the use of ground lines to help horse and rider find the right takeoff points. When you set a course at home, always adjust the distances to be appropriate for the horse and rider schooling them (refer to the generally accepted distance ranges listed on p. 25).

short, or ideal distance. An ideal distance is the place where the horse can leave the ground allowing him to create the most efficient *bascule* (geometric curve) over a particular obstacle (see p. 27).

The bascule bridge (or drawbridge) has a counterweight that continuously balances the length, or span, of the bridge as it rises or lowers. Likewise, when jumping, the horse first shifts his weight to his hindquarters as a counterweight as he pushes off from the ground. This allows the horse to rise up through his back and lift and tuck his front legs in order to clear the height of the obstacle. The horse's arc peaks when his withers are at the highest point over the fence. Then, by stretching

his neck forward and down, the horse creates the counterweight needed to land safely, and in balance, on the other side.

If a horse leaves the ground from a *long distance*, it means that he left the ground a little farther away from the base of the jump than what would be ideal. Leaving from what's often called a "long spot" flattens the horse's arc over the fence because he will have to reach out horizontally in order to clear the width of the obstacle. Because the arc is flatter, the apex of the bascule will be later, resulting in a longer landing distance. A really long spot draws gasps from the spectators, as it is often very apparent the horse may not be able to clear the width of the obstacle.

If the horse leaves from a *short distance* it means he has gotten a little too close to the base of the fence, and perhaps even added an extra stride in the line or combination. This is referred to as a "chip" or "leaving from a deep spot" and requires the horse to expend more energy vertically in order to clear the fence. Leaving from a short distance moves the apex

> ▶ This is a standard 60-foot line, which for hunter and equitation riders, would be generally ridden in four strides. In the jumper ring it is left up to the rider to decide how many strides to ride in the lines and combinations. As a rider advances she should practice riding this line not only in a *slightly forward four strides* (it will ride long because it is set up in an indoor arena), but also in *five medium strides*, and in *six collected strides*, in order to practice adjustability. This illustrates that the physical measurement for distances may not directly correlate to a hard-and-fast number of strides. It is the pace, length of stride, and quality of the canter that determines the optimum number of strides that should be ridden between related elements.

of the bascule closer to the takeoff spot, resulting in a steeper angle over the fence, and a landing that is closer to the fence on the backside. Furthermore, if the rider asks the horse to take off so close to the base of the fence that the jump is entirely out of the horse's field of vision (see the discussion on the horse's perspective, beginning on p. 7).

MEASURING A DISTANCE

Distance is also the term used to refer to *the measurement, in either feet or meters, between related obstacles*. When you are talking about distance in regards to a jump course, you are most likely using this definition. This physical measurement, which is noted on the course diagram posted at the in-gate for all obstacles with related distances of 90 feet or less (it is optional for the course designer to post distances in excess of 90 feet), is converted by the rider into a corresponding number of strides that a horse should take between those related obstacles. The number of strides is calculated by taking the physical measurement between the two obstacles, subtracting 12 feet (the generally accepted guideline for the space needed for landing and takeoff), and then dividing the remainder by 12 feet.

Educated riders can look at a course diagram or walk a course and easily convert the physical measurement into a number of strides. When developing their plan for how they will ride the course, riders refer to the distance between related obstacles as a one-, two-, or three-stride combination, or a four-, five-, or six-stride line (for example), rather than quoting a physical distance measurement.

And, just as the takeoff point can be *long*, *short*, or *ideal*, lines and combinations often have the descriptor of *long* (forward), *short* (collected) or *medium* ("easy"). When the physical measurement of a line results in something *less* than an equal number of 12-foot strides the line will be a little short. Conversely, when there is a remainder *over* an equal number of 12-foot strides, the line will ride slightly long. These descriptors actually refer to the pace, or the quality of the canter, and the corresponding length of stride that is needed to accurately negotiate the line or combination in order to arrive at the correct takeoff point for each obstacle.

Originally, stridecounting was a tool that helped beginning riders judge the quality of their canter so as to arrive at an ideal takeoff point in front of a fence. This practice evolved into a requirement at horse shows to "ride the numbers," in part because jumping courses began to be held in arenas with smaller square footage and a perimeter fence. This is in contrast with jumping competitions from days gone by where the courses were jumped in an open field over varied terrain, and where a "good gallop" such as one would carry when foxhunting was what was needed to meet the fences properly. The smaller footprint of today's riding arenas requires more

V All distances included in the course diagrams in this book are set for horses. When schooling ponies be sure to take the difference in stride length into consideration. Here I have included the pony distance recommendations that appear in the USHJA Trainer Certification Manual. Note that the USHJA recommends that pony riders practice riding lines set for horses and learn to fit an even number of strides within that distance.

DISTANCES FOR PONIES

Strides	Small	Medium	Large
1	20'	22'	24'
2	30'	32'	34'
3	39'	41'- 42'	45'
4	48'- 50'	52'- 53'	56'
5	58'- 61'	62'- 64'	67'- 68'
6	68'- 71'	72'- 74'	78'- 80'
7	78'- 80'	82'- 84'	89'- 91'

accuracy in order to meet the shorter distances between obstacles, and knowing how physical distances translate into a corresponding stride count helps with the negotiation of a course. In the hunter and equitation divisions, there can be heavy penalties if a rider either adds or leaves out a stride in a line or combination.

FACTORS THAT AFFECT DISTANCE

Distances are affected by many factors, such as the course design itself, the condition of the footing, weather conditions, and the slope of the arena. The horse's natural jumping ability and stride length, as well his adjustability, has an influence on how distances are met. Perhaps the most significant factor is the way in which a rider approaches a fence, either in terms of the quality of the canter achieved or the angle of the track the rider chooses to take. The rider must practice the ability to create the optimum forward and balanced canter so she can ride up to the distance, whether it be medium, slightly long, or slightly short.

DISTANCE RANGES

When building schooling exercises and courses your goal is to avoid anything "trappy" or unsafe. The tables and illustrations in this section provide you with ranges for distances between related obstacles that are generally accepted as appropriate, helping you avoid setting any distances that will "ride on the half-stride"—that is, either 6 feet shorter or longer than the standard range.

When setting an exercise or a course to be used primarily for beginning riders or green horses (with low fences), or when schooling horses short on scope (that is, those with a stride length less than a normal 12 feet), set the obstacles toward the shorter end of the distance ranges. Also, courses set up indoors tend to require slightly shorter distances because the smaller square-footage and tighter corners in an indoor arena tend to slow down the horse's forward motion and shorten the length of the horse's stride. However, it is important to remember that in competition, distances are set for horses with a normal to big stride (12 to 13 feet), so beginner riders and shorter-strided horses do need to practice a more forward pace so they can meet the distances they will encounter at a show.

When jumping 3 feet to 3 feet 6 inches, set schooling fences toward the middle of the recommended distance range. For jumps higher than that, related distances should run toward the upper end of the ranges (or perhaps even a little longer).

RELATED DISTANCES

When setting up *combinations*—that is, two or more obstacles with three strides or less between them—it

DISTANCE CHART

1 The minimum distances contained in the chart on this page are appropriate for fences with a height of 3 feet. The maximum distances are more typical for a 4-foot course. One pace is equal to one human 3-foot step (or one yard).

2 The chart shows distances for horses (with a 12- to 13-foot stride) jumping an outside course. Distances should be adjusted (shortened) about 4 feet for small ponies (a 9- to 10-foot stride) or you can simply add an extra stride when the lines are set at the minimum distances. For medium ponies (a 10- to 11-foot stride), shorten the lines anywhere from 2 to 8 feet, or set the fences so it is again comfortable for the pony to simply add one full stride in the line. For large ponies (11- to 12-foot stride), the minimum distance measurement may be used, assuming the pony carries a fairly forward pace.

3 When trotting into a line, the line will ride a minimum of 3 feet longer. Typically, when trotting into a line the horse takes one additional canter stride between the elements.

4 There are a number of factors that cause a line to ride shorter or longer, so adjust your lines to fit specific conditions. For example:

• **Lines ride shorter** (because the horse's stride tends to lengthen) by at least a foot when: the arena is large and open; the horse is galloping fast; there is a downhill line; you are riding the inside track of a broken or bending line; or you are on the last line of the course and going toward "home" or the in-gate.

• **Lines ride longer** (because the horse's stride tends to shorten) by at least a foot when: the conditions are muddy; the arena has deep or soft footing; the jumping arena is small; the line is uphill; the jump is after a tight turn or rollback: the jumps are big, spooky, solid, or airy; or you are jumping away from "home" or away from the direction of the in-gate.

5 The type of fence used and its order in the sequence of a line affects the distances. A vertical-to-vertical line rides as a shorter distance than a vertical-to-oxer, for example. (See pp. 26-29 for details on how the type of fence affects how a distance will ride.)

6 The longer the distance between the fences, the more room there is for adjustment on the rider's part. Shorter distances and combinations require a greater degree of accuracy in course design and setup.

TROT/CANTER AND PLACING POLES

		PACES	FEET
Trotting Poles	Min	1.5	4'
	Max	2	5.5'
Canter Poles	Min	3	9'
	Max	3.5	10'
Placing Pole Front of Fence (Cantering)	Min	3	9'
	Max	3.5	10'
Placing Pole After a Fence (Cantering)	Min	3.5	10'

The recommended minimum and maximum number of human paces and physical measurement when setting ground poles.

BETWEEN FENCES AT A CANTER

		PACES	FEET
Bounce	Min	3.5	10'
	Max	4	12'
One Stride	Min	8	24'
	Max	9	28'
Two Strides	Min	11	33'
	Max	13	39'
Three Strides	Min	18	24'
	Max	17	52'
Four Strides	Min	20	60'
	Max	22	65'
Five Strides	Min	24	72'
	Max	26	78'
Six Strides	Min	28	84'
	Max	30	90'
Seven Strides	Min	32	96'
	Max	35	105'

The recommended minimum and maximum number of human paces and physical measurement when setting related fences.

STRIDE CHARTS COURTESY OF CHRYSTINE TAUBER AND USHJA

	Vertical	Square Oxer	Ascending Oxer	Triple Bar
Vertical	25′	24′	23′	22′
Square Oxer	26′	25′	24′	23′
Ascending Oxer	27′	26′	25′	24′
Triple Bar	28′	27′	26′	not recommended

(SECOND FENCE — row axis label)

∧ I based this chart on FEI recommendations, providing the distances for a one-stride combination between different types of fences. Distances are measured from the back rail of the first fence to the front rail of the second fence. Add 11 feet to the distances for a two-stride combination, and 22 feet for a three-stride combination. For a line that is four strides or longer, add 12 feet for each additional stride when fences are up to 3 feet in height. For fences higher than 3 feet and up to 3½ feet in height, add 13 feet for each additional stride. When the fences are over 4 feet, you may need to add up to 14 feet for each additional stride.

is important to consider the construction of the fences involved. When setting *lines*—two related jumps placed four or more strides apart—the distance isn't as important. Many courses have a line that leads into a combination, or a combination that leads into to a line, that is set a little "long" or a little "short." This is a test of your horse's adjustability.

These *related distances* are always measured from the *back* rail of the first fence to the *front* vertical plane of the second fence. At a horse show, the physical measurement between related elements in the class should be included on the course diagram posted at the in-gate. You need to understand what the distances mean so that you can

correctly answer the questions on course. Jumper and equitation riders, in particular, need to know how to vary related distances in their practice courses at home so they can be prepared for these questions in competition.

TAKEOFF AND LANDING DISTANCES FOR DIFFERENT TYPES OF FENCES

A horse's bascule (as discussed earlier, the geometric curve the horse travels when jumping a fence), is different for different types of fences. This geometry affects both the takeoff point and landing distance. In addition to how the terrain and/or footing affects the horse's stride length, and the combination of and related distance(s) between fences, different fence types either add to or decrease the difficulty of the course and how a rider plans to ride it. It is also true that takeoff and landing distances increase as the height of the obstacle increases or as the horse picks up speed; therefore, when bigger fences are used in a line or combination, the length of the combination/line needs to be increased accordingly.

	Standard Distance	Long Distance	Short Distance	Half Stride
Two Stride	36′	39′- 42′	30′- 33′	<30 or >42
Three Stride	48′	51′- 54′	42′- 45′	<42 or >54
Four Stride	60′	63′- 66′	54′- 57′	<54 or >66
Five Stride	72′	75′- 78′	66′- 69′	<66 or >78

∧ Related distances between elements in combinations and lines.

VERTICALS

The apex of the bascule over a vertical is directly over the front plane of the jump. Both the takeoff and landing distance is 6 feet, assuming a

12-foot stride length or equal distance on the front and back side of a vertical fence. Vertical fences are easy to negotiate when the horse can leave from a normal or long spot. Horses can have rails down when they get "too deep" to a vertical (that is, too close to the base of the fence at takeoff).

SQUARE OXERS

The apex of the bascule over a square oxer is directly in the center between the two sets of standards. The arc of the bascule is slightly flatter than the arc for a vertical fence, and the landing point is closer to the back rail of the fence, as compared to landing after a vertical. Oxers "slow" a horse in the air, which can help to collect the horse upon landing. It is better to take off at a normal to deep spot when jumping an oxer.

ASCENDING OXERS

The apex of the bascule over an ascending oxer is just short of the back rail. The arc of the bascule is steeper than the arc over a

> The takeoff and landing distances for a vertical, square oxer, ascending oxer, and triple bar. The apex of the bascule of each jump is marked by the "X."

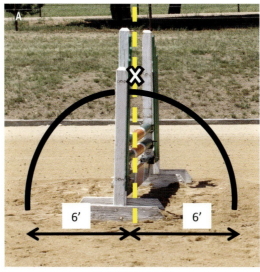

VERTICAL FENCE

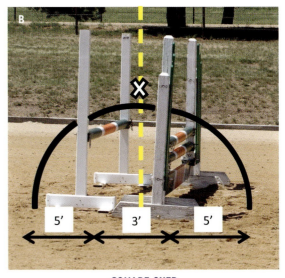

SQUARE OXER

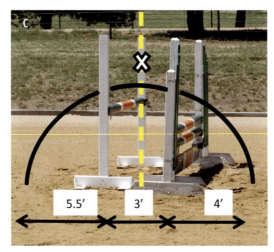

ASCENDING OXER

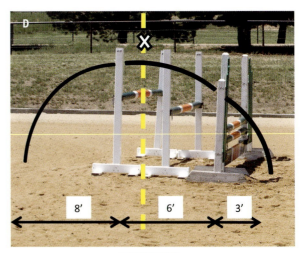

TRIPLE BAR

Here we see the same 48-foot combination with different fence types incorporated. The vertical to vertical in Photo A rides in three, nice, easy 12-foot strides. The vertical to oxer in Photo B rides as a slightly longer distance because the takeoff point for the second fence (the oxer) is closer to the base of the fence than for the vertical. This means that the distance for the combination either needs to be shortened 1½ feet (from 48 to 46½ feet), or the horse needs to take slightly longer strides than the standard 12-foot stride in order to get to the correct (closer) takeoff point for the second fence. The oxer to oxer in Photo C rides even longer because the landing point after the first oxer is closer to the base on the backside than for a vertical. The takeoff point for the second oxer is closer to the base, too, so the 48-foot distance must be "made up" by lengthening the horse's stride, or the distance in the combination needs to be shortened by 3 feet (from 48 to 45 feet). Remember that in addition, oxers tend to "slow" the impulsion of the horse and cause the horse to shorten the length of the first stride after landing.

square oxer. This means the horse will land farther away from the back rail, just not quite as far away as when landing after a vertical.

TRIPLE BARS

The apex of the bascule over a triple bar is above the back rail. The arc of the bascule is much longer and flatter than either the vertical or oxer fences. A triple bar encourages the horse to lengthen in the air, resulting in a longer stride upon landing. Collection is difficult when landing and going away from a triple bar. The lower the front vertical plane of the fence is in comparison to the overall height of the jump, the closer the horse should take off from the base. This type of fence is best jumped from a deep spot.

FENCE TYPE AND THE HORSE'S FORWARD MOTION

Although lines and combinations are generally assumed to be ridden in equal stride lengths, in reality, upon landing, the first stride the horse takes going away from the jump is slightly shorter than the subsequent strides, because the trajectory of the jump slows the horse's forward motion. As the overall size of the obstacle increases (both width and height), the increased trajectory of the wider/higher obstacle will proportionately decrease the horse's forward motion. The course designer needs to consider how much to adjust standard distances when setting the course in order to compensate for this loss of forward motion.

Different types of fences also cause a line or combination to ride shorter or longer. The more strides between fences, the less fence type impacts how the horse meets each jump; however, when shorter distances are used, fence construction can lengthen or shorten the distance the horse has to travel by as little as 6 inches up to as much as 6 feet. This can make a line that measured as a "normal distance" actually ride on the half-stride. Lines and combinations with the exact same measurement can ride very differently, depending upon what type of fences are used, how the horse meets and leaves those fences, and whether they increase or decrease the horse's forward motion as he goes over them.

3

THE THEORY BEHIND
COURSE DESIGN

- **Jump Courses for Schooling vs. Showing**
- **The Art of Course Design**
- **The Geometry of Course Design**
- **Levels of Difficulty from Basic to Technical**
- **Getting Started**
- **Quick Reference: Nine Considerations When Designing a Jump Course**

JUMP COURSES FOR SCHOOLING VS. SHOWING

Fences and courses set at home are meant to provide a safe and meaningful learning experience for you and your horse. In training scenarios, you have the luxury of being able to move and adjust jumps as needed. At a horse show, though, you have to live with the way a course is set. The course designer plans and sets the course to test the competing horses and riders abilities against each other. All competitors in a class are given the opportunity to answer the same set of questions better than their fellow competitors. That is why, once a class has started at a horse show, the jumps will not be moved.

Horse show courses are designed to ask questions in accordance with horse show rules and the appropriate skill level expected for a particular division. The course designer assumes that the horses and riders electing to compete in a class recognize, understand, and are capable of performing the skills necessary to negotiate a particular course successfully. This is why your education in jumping needs to include an under-

Beautiful, flowing jump courses don't just happen. A great course will always follow the basic principles of design and the rules of geometry. Course design is a creative art, but it must still conform to the limitations of equine biomechanics and the rules and laws of mathematical science.

standing of the fundamentals of course design so you can at least recognize the questions before you have to jump them. Nothing helps you accomplish this better than physically setting up jump exercises and courses yourself, and then riding them. (Note: I do recommend having qualified professional oversight when first learning to set a course or other jump exercises. In the case of working without a trainer present, you should practice setting and riding exercises and courses using only poles on the ground.)

Whether you school at home because you just love to jump or because you want to prepare to answer questions that might be asked when "taking the test" at a horse show, this section will help you develop an understanding of the theory behind jump course design.

COURSE DESIGN OBJECTIVES

Because this guide is about designing and building jump courses for use in schooling, some of the design considerations differ from the objectives that a course designer considers when planning courses for competition. First of all, when designing courses for schooling purposes at a training facility, you need to accommodate a "broader audience." At large barns and boarding facilities, you may have other riders who wish to school your course, and their skill level may range from beginner to advanced, from casual riders to elite competitors. Their area of interest may be in hunters, jumpers, or equitation. This means the number and placement of jumps in a good schooling course will need to be set so that a very simple course can be ridden, but with just a few alterations, the course can ask technical questions, as well.

The objective when setting a jump course at home or at the barn where you ride is simplicity and versatility. You want to design a course with the jumps placed so that a minimum amount of time and effort is required to adjust them in order to school different exercises. Schooling courses are often left up for a period of time, so you should set your fences so there is enough room

> A sample jump course diagram.

to do flatwork around them, and to maneuver the equipment used to water and drag the footing. Generally in schooling scenarios you do not set jumps up against the rail, as might be done at a horse show, and this limits your design options.

Schooling courses ideally should have more obstacles than you would need for any one course so that you will have options to create multiple courses and/or exercises, without having to move jumps very far before you reset for the next course. If you have a limited jump inventory or if you are working in a small space, your course may have fewer elements than what you would see at a horse show, and as such you may have to do more alterations to your course before you completely reset your next course. Whatever you set, you will probably want to include some simple fences that can be easily altered into a gymnastic or grid. You never know when you might need to set something like this in order to fix a problem a horse or rider may be having.

Other differences include less fill and/or fewer decorations. At home you won't be trying to impress spectators, and you probably won't be concerned about where the first and last fence on your course will be placed in terms of getting horses in and out of the ring in order to keep the horse show on schedule. Schooling courses are designed purely as training exercises and, if possible, you will want to mix up the types of elements included on your course so it includes both hunter and jumper type fences. This way, both riders and their horses are accustomed to a variety of elements, and prepared for just about any scenario at a horse show.

THE ART OF COURSE DESIGN

Just like designing a building that is functional or drawing a furniture plan that flows, designing a jump course will follow the same general design principals. Essentially, any design process is an exercise in problem solving, using a few fundamental concepts. Design principals are used to organize or arrange structural elements that, in our case, are obstacles to be jumped. The principals of design include: *balance, proportion, rhythm, emphasis,* and *unity.* Here is how they apply to course design:

• **Balance** is the concept of visual equilibrium. The obstacles/elements of a course should be balanced equally throughout the arena, avoiding a concentration of fences at one end or on one side of the ring. You also want to plan for balance between right- and left-lead fences, and create a balance between vertical and spread obstacles.

• **Proportion** refers to the relative size and scale of the various elements in the design. In course design, it is important to be aware of the size and scale of your fences in proportion to the size of your arena. Using massive wings and big chunky boxes in a small arena

doesn't allow much space for anything else. However, using 8- to 10-foot poles in a small arena gives you room to set a course that is useful. Addressing proportion in course design also relates to keeping the elements of your lines and/or combinations proportional in terms of color and mass so that they are easy to identify as related obstacles.

• **Rhythm** is the timed movement through space on an easily connected path. The presence of rhythm creates predictability and order in a composition. Rhythm depends largely upon the elements of a pattern: linear, repetitive, or alternating. *Linear rhythm* refers to the characteristics of an individual line, which may be straight, curved, circular, or semicircular. *Repetitive rhythm* involves the use of a pattern to achieve a visual "beat," which is a characteristic of gymnastics and combinations. *Alternative rhythm* is created through a specific pattern in which items are presented in alternating fashion, such as long/short/long, vertical/oxer/vertical, or side/diagonal/side.

• **Emphasis** is often referred to by artists as the "point of focus." It marks the location in a composition that most strongly draws the viewer's attention. All riders look for a focal point when negotiating the track that they will take to a fence. In course design, you want to insure that you do, in fact, have a clear point of emphasis for each fence, line, or combination, and that there is no interference with getting to the point of emphasis (the jump). In course design, you also want to be aware of both intentional and un-intentional emphasis. A course designer may intentionally create a distraction for the horse, such as bright colors or unusual shapes in a jumper or high level equitation classes. But emphasis that is un-intentionally created, such as sun spots in an indoor arena or decorations blowing in the wind, serve no useful purpose and the course designer will need to compensate for, or eliminate, any type of unwanted emphasis whenever possible.

• **Unity** is the underlying principal that summarizes all the elements of design. It refers to the coherence of the whole, or the sense that all of the parts are working together to achieve harmony. Unity can be achieved through pattern, the consistent use of form and color, or a common quality of style or purpose. For courses at home, especially if you are trying to use both jumper- and hunter-type elements, you will want to unify your course through the use of pattern (rhythm) and color.

THE GEOMETRY OF COURSE DESIGN

A jumping course consists of both straight and curved lines with obstacles placed along the way. The horse is physically built to travel in a straight line. His spine is fairly rigid and supported by very strong back muscles that are

not very flexible (part of the reason why we can sit on them). This helps explain why a horse jumps his best when he is allowed to jump a fence perpendicular to his center. Keeping the horse's body straight upon the approach to the jump, in the air, and upon landing gives him the best chance to maintain his natural balance, which in turn will result in a flowing forward round without faults.

Designing a course to meet these objectives means that you have to plan your course so that there is adequate room to travel to the jumps, and you must set related obstacles square so the horse can stay on a straight line to jump them (see p. 40). You need to have the jumps set at the correct angle(s) to each other so that the line through the middle of the jump(s) easily follows the track the horse is meant to take on his approach to each fence, and that he should take upon landing.

Good course design relies heavily on the use of flat shapes, including lines and circles, that are then "contained" within a fixed space—in other words, within the boundaries of your arena. In order to plan and draw a course properly, you need a rudimentary, or at least an intuitive, understanding of the mathematical subject called *plane geometry*. Geometry is the study of the properties, relationships, and measurements of points, lines, curves, and surfaces.

THREE BASIC GEOMETRIC PRINCIPLES

This book isn't a course on mathematics, but having some understanding of how the basic relationships of line and space apply to course design will help you understand why some tracks and jump placement(s) "work" and others do not. I have never found it easy to see the angles and tracks to the fence. When I tried to put a course design on paper for the first time, I struggled with these basics. However, it does get easier with time.

I had the most difficulty figuring out the correct angle of the fences and the correct corresponding lead so that the horse would be capable of traveling in balance. When you draw, or place, a fence on your course with an incorrect angle, you can create an awkward track or even make the approach to the fence impossible. This section of the book focuses on the three basic geometric principles you need to make the courses you design comfortable for the horse and rider. At the same time, you'll learn the factors that can make your course more challenging while remaining fair.

The three basic geometric principles include:

1 Determining the best direction for the track around your course so the horse has the best chance to land in balance and maintain forward motion.

2 Drawing, or setting, a track that allows the horse to jump over the middle of all fences in a line or combination. In other words, keeping your lines "square."

3 Determining the correct angles for placing the fences on your course so that the course flows through the corners and any turns can be ridden smoothly and in balance.

Course design isn't easy, so expect to learn from your mistakes. Even the best course designers sometimes have to make "course corrections" when they actually start to build their courses in an arena.

LEVELS OF DIFFICULTY FROM BASIC TO TECHNICAL

COURSES FOR GENERAL USE

When designing a course for general use, keep in mind the skill required to successfully "answer certain types of questions" (clear certain obstacles, negotiate complex tracks, demonstrate your horse's stride adjustability). Always consider the "end users" because, especially at a

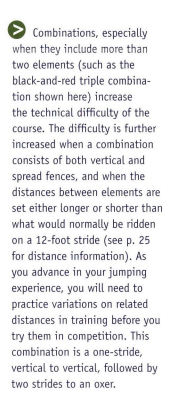

> Combinations, especially when they include more than two elements (such as the black-and-red triple combination shown here) increase the technical difficulty of the course. The difficulty is further increased when a combination consists of both vertical and spread fences, and when the distances between elements are set either longer or shorter than what would normally be ridden on a 12-foot stride (see p. 25 for distance information). As you advance in your jumping experience, you will need to practice variations on related distances in training before you try them in competition. This combination is a one-stride, vertical to vertical, followed by two strides to an oxer.

busy boarding or training stable, other trainers or riders should not have to take components apart and/or move fences around in order to use them in their own schooling program. This defeats the purpose of designing the course in the first place. Your goal should be to include design variety and offer challenges, while at the same ensuring you do not overface the majority of horses and riders. Avoid anything that is "trappy" or potentially unsafe.

When you are designing a course that you know will be used primarily for beginners, increase the number of strides in the lines if you have the space to do so. Focus on the use of single verticals, allowing trainers and instructors the opportunity to further break down the fences to cross-rails or poles on the ground at the beginning of lessons and build the jumps back up as their students are ready to move on. Having more single fences with less fill makes it a lot easier to set the fence in a way that is useful and saves wear and tear on superfluous components.

WHAT MAKES A COURSE HARD?

What makes a course harder (or easier) is generally related to *track*, not the jump itself. Although height and spread do play a factor, what increases the technicality of a course is:

- The angle of the track that is required in the approach to a fence.
- The inclusion of rollbacks (see p. 17).

- Increasing the number of changes in direction.
- The inclusion of bending or broken lines.
- Varying the distance between elements in a line or in a combination to a stride length that is either longer or shorter than the standard 12-foot stride.
- The related or unrelated distances between fences.
- Increasing the number of fences.
- Choosing certain components in the construction of each fence.

A straight line approach to a single fence, or into a line that has a straight track, requires only basic skill to execute. To simplify further, the longer the approach to the fence, or line, the more time the rider has to get the horse on the appropriate track (perpendicular to center) to the fence and establish the necessary forward pace.

Diagonal lines are a little trickier. Visually, it takes slightly more skill to "see" the track that will be needed so that you do not turn too early (or too late) in order to get the horse straight to the jump.

Combinations are considered more technical, especially when there are more than two elements. The shorter the distance between elements in a combination, the more accuracy is required.

Both bending and broken lines are considered technical, as are angled lines. Angled lines are most often seen in the higher level jumpers; when riding for time in a jump-off; when demonstrating "handiness" in a hunter or

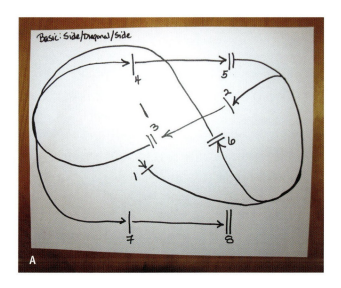

Basic: Side/Diagonal/Side

A

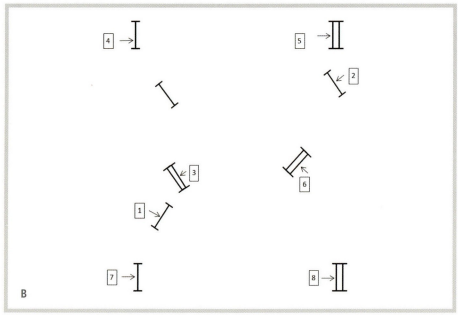

B

> The plan for a jump course starts with the design of a track, here shown on paper (A) and using a computer program (B).

equitation round; or when demonstrating "brilliance" in a hunter derby class. Generally speaking, the rider makes *a choice* to take an angled track rather than the course requiring it.

GETTING STARTED

The plan for a jump course starts with the design of a track. Once you have a general idea of how your track will flow around the arena, then you can add the jumps. A course should travel across the entire space available, have approximately the same number of fences off both leads, and have an equal distribution between vertical and spread fences. The primary objectives of a good course include:

- Free-flowing forward movement for the entire course, including turns.
- Appropriate distances between obstacles.
- Smooth change(s) of rein.

THE TRACK

As mentioned, a jump course is basically made up of straight tracks and tracks that are circular, semicircular, or slightly curved. The size of your ring, both the length and the width, will set the outside boundaries for your course and will determine how long your lines can be and how wide you can make the turns. There is no rea-

A course is determined by the track(s) that you choose to use and consists of straight lines and curved lines that are limited by the space you have available and the skill level of the horse/rider expected to negotiate them. Horses retain balance and forward motion better when they can travel in straight lines or those with a gradual bend. The tighter the turn, the more a horse has to work to stabilize his body, and the harder it is to re-establish forward motion. Your track(s) should allow adequate room for turns and for re-engaging the canter following them.

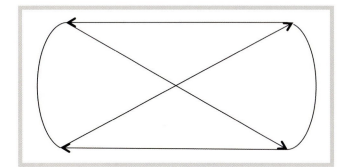

The track design for beginners and the majority of hunter courses follows a side/diagonal/side pattern. These courses always begin with a single vertical fence. The turns should be wide (ideally the width of the arena) and the approach to each obstacle as long as possible and in proportion to the distance provided upon landing. You want to give the rider plenty of room to re-establish pace, change leads, and make any other necessary adjustment(s) in order to have a straight approach to the next fence.

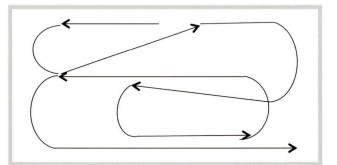

The track design for handy hunters, equitation classes, and jumpers should include more turns, including rollbacks, and can also feature bending and/or broken lines. The radius of the turns should be a minimum of 25 feet (see p. 45). Ideally you should allow for *at least* three straight strides for the approach to any single fence, line, or combination.

son not to utilize all of the space available to you, so try to design your track so it travels across and through the entire space. Keep in mind that wider, more sweeping turns create smoother rounds. The more advanced the rider and the more schooling the horse has had, the more turns you can include in the course and the tighter you can make the track.

HOW TO PLACE YOUR FIRST FENCE ON COURSE

How the rider approaches the first fence is important for establishing the pace that should be maintained for the remainder of the course. In training scenarios, you can start on any fence, and in fact, you should practice all the possible placements so that you are prepared for whatever may be set by the course designer when you go to a show.

Where you place the first fence should take into account the ring size, topography (inclines/declines), location of in-gate, length of approach, whether it is a vertical or spread, whether it is a single fence or part of a line, and how it is built. Remember the characteristics of a good course (see p. 33) and choose to place your first fence so you can meet your course goals.

Course Design Orientation

The orientation of the course you design should match the orientation of your arena as it would typically be viewed from the vantage point of the in-gate (vertically or horizontally).

I always have to double-check my drawings to make sure that I haven't angled the fences improperly, resulting in an awkward turn or creating a drawing that no one can follow. I have found that the easiest way for me to find the correct angle for the first fence (and others) is to look at the *track* the horse will take across the middle of the fence and from there envision a turn with ample space on the correct lead. The correct lead for the first fence is determined by the course design's orientation to the in-gate (horizontal or vertical).

When the course design (and your arena orientation according to the in-gate) is *horizontal*, whichever *lower* corner the track points to is the correct lead for the first fence (so if the track points to the lower left corner, the first fence should be jumped off the left lead). When the course design is drawn according to a *vertical* orientation, the correct angle when drawing the first jump on course is still determined by track the horse will take across the middle of the fence but, in this case, whichever *upper* corner the track points to is the correct lead for the fence. Take a look at the sample drawings I've included here and notice how when the drawing is rotated and orientation changes, your point of view changes, too.

CROSS-MEASURING TO KEEP YOUR STRAIGHT LINES SQUARE

One of the most critical aspects of course design is to keep lines or combinations "square" to allow the horse to travel

Placing Your First Fence

First Fence — Short Approach on a Diagonal Track — Can be jumped either direction. As drawn, this fence has a short approach out of a corner going away from the In-Gate, so it will be little harder to establish pace than it would be if there was a longer approach.

First Fence — Straight Track — Can be jumped either direction and off of either lead. In this case, the arrow indicates that it would jumped off of the Left Lead.

First Fence — Long Approach on a Diagonal Track — Can be jumped from either direction. As drawn, this fence has a nice long approach so there is plenty of time to establish pace. The direction is away from the In Gate, which may make it harder for the rider to establish a forward pace.

First Fence — Assume for this example that the ring has significant slope downhill. Starting the course going downhill and toward the In-Gate on a straight track will help encourage a forward pace.

First Fence — Assume, for this example, that the ring has significant slope uphill. Starting the course going uphill, going away from the In-Gate and on a spread fence, will require a concerted effort to establish the appropriate forward pace.

First Fence — Starting the course on a diagonal line off a short corner, will require a balanced turn and a forward steady pace through the corner and into the line so that the number of strides in the line can be met easily.

IN GATE

 Six examples of "first fences" and the qualities that determine whether they are easy, moderately difficult, or challenging.

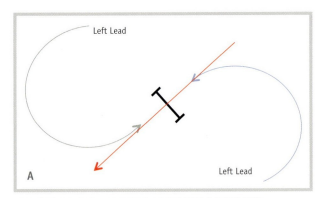

> Horizontal Course Design Orientation: A diagonal single fence set off the left lead (A) and off the right lead (B).

DIAGONAL SINGLE SET OFF OF THE LEFT LEAD

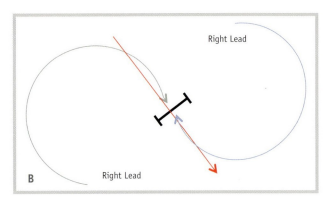

DIAGONAL SINGLE SET OFF OF THE RIGHT LEAD

> Vertical Course Design Orientation: A diagonal single fence set off the left lead (A) and off the right lead (B).

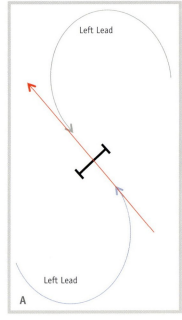

DIAGONAL SINGLE SET OFF OF THE LEFT LEAD

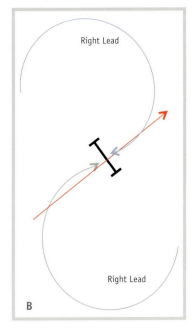

DIAGONAL SINGLE SET OFF OF THE RIGHT LEAD

on a straight track over the center of the related obstacles. A method called *cross-measuring* can be used to ensure the lines you plan on paper or set on your jump course are square. First measure the appropriate length of the line for the number of strides that you have planned for your course (see p. 33 for details on distances). You do this by measuring down the middle of the line, as well as from outside standard to outside standard and inside standard to inside standard. Next, check to see that the line is square by measuring diagonally from the inside standard of the first jump, across to the outside standard of the second jump, then from the outside standard of the first jump to the inside standard of the second jump. The two diagonal measurements need to be the same. When one of the diagonals measures longer than the other, push/ rotate the corners of the outside standard of the side with the longer measurement toward the opposite inside

You need to understand how to cross-measure for "straightness" for all course elements placed on a straight line, such as lines and combinations (A). When fences are not placed so they are square, you unintentionally create awkward angles to your track. It is often hard to "see" squareness, so you do need to use a tape measure when setting lines and combinations, measuring from the standard of one obstacle to the opposite standard of the jump that follows (in blue), repeating the process for the other side (in red), and making sure the distances are equal (B).

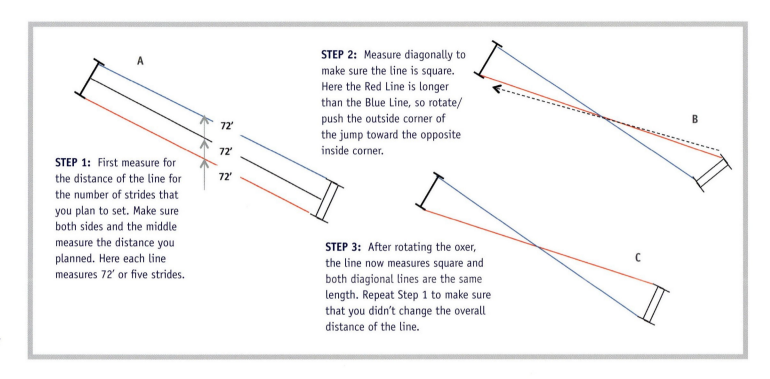

STEP 1: First measure for the distance of the line for the number of strides that you plan to set. Make sure both sides and the middle measure the distance you planned. Here each line measures 72' or five strides.

STEP 2: Measure diagonally to make sure the line is square. Here the Red Line is longer than the Blue Line, so rotate/push the outside corner of the jump toward the opposite inside corner.

STEP 3: After rotating the oxer, the line now measures square and both diagonal lines are the same length. Repeat Step 1 to make sure that you didn't change the overall distance of the line.

A 72' 72' 72' B C

> Three steps to make sure your lines are square.

standard until both the diagonal measurements are the same. Here's a tip: You need to rotate/move the standard by one-half the difference in measurement between the two diagonals. So, for example, when the difference in the measurement between the two diagonal lengths is 4 inches, you need to rotate the outside standard in by 2 inches to make the line square.

CIRCLES, TURNS, AND ANGLES
Including Circles and Turns in Your Course
Earlier in this section I mentioned that because the

horse's spine is fairly rigid, he physically cannot move on a perfect circle. His strides are essentially taken in a straight line, and he adapts his movement to a curved line by side-stepping a little each stride. When the horse is well-schooled, this adaptation is negligible to the human eye. The horse also uses his neck (which is very flexible) as a balance mechanism during a turn, just as he does when jumping a fence. Because the rider asks the horse's neck to flex slightly to the inside when traveling around a curved line, the horse needs to lift and shift his ribcage to the outside of the bend as a counterweight in order to

maintain his balance. This creates the "bend" that we see in the horse's body as he moves through a circle or turn.

The limited range of lateral motion in the horse's spine makes it difficult for the horse to achieve a uniform bend around a complete circle with a diameter of 40 to 50 feet (a 12- to 15-meter circle) or less. Assuming that the horse maintains a 12-foot stride, a 12- to 15-meter circle would be ridden in about 13 strides when traveling around the full circumference (360 degrees), which translates to a track of 155 to 160 feet.

To incorporate a comfortable yet tight semicircle or turn in your course, you need to allow the horse enough room to take six to seven strides between elements (a total distance of at least 72 to 84 feet), plus the distance needed for landing and takeoff (when a jump is involved.) Smaller circles and semicircles, and tighter turns are proportionately harder and require that more of the horse's weight be shifted to his hindquarters for stability, resulting in the shortening of stride and length of his frame. Remember your goal is to encourage a forward, flowing track—small circles and tight turns are contrary to this ideal.

With all this in mind, plan for as much room as you can for circles, turns, and changes of direction. Ensure there is sufficient space after every obstacle for the horse to land, change leads if need be, and then re-establish his canter before he has to jump the next obstacle. For beginners, green horses, and most hunter-type courses,

use the entire width of the ring for your turns. For handy hunter, equitation, and jumper courses, you can include more and tighter turns—just keep in mind you still want them to ride safely. Plan to have a minimum of three strides on approach to a fence and three strides after landing.

Setting Related Fences with Correct Angles

Setting related fences at angles that are *at least* 180 degrees to each other makes the approach to the next jump, as well as the subsequent track that you take when you land and canter away from it, much easier. Wider angles allow you a much better chance of setting your horse up to be straight to the second jump (perpendicu-

V This drawing shows the minimum arc that you should allow for when planning semicircles and turns, unless you have the space available to allow for a very long approach to the second fence.

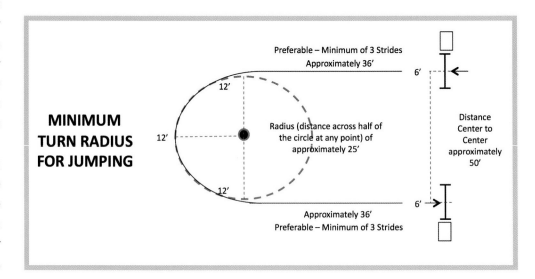

MINIMUM TURN RADIUS FOR JUMPING

Preferable – Minimum of 3 Strides
Approximately 36'

12'

12'

Radius (distance across half of the circle at any point) of approximately 25'

12'

Approximately 36'
Preferable – Minimum of 3 Strides

6'

6'

Distance Center to Center approximately 50'

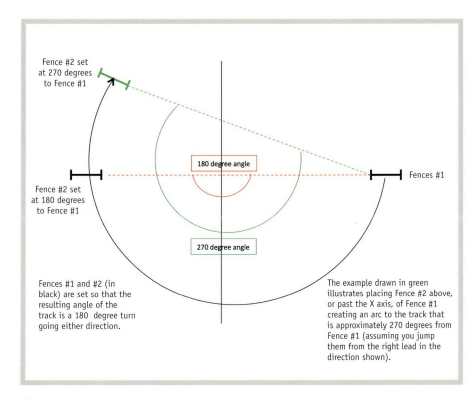

Fence #2 set at 270 degrees to Fence #1

Fence #2 set at 180 degrees to Fence #1

180 degree angle

270 degree angle

Fences #1

Fences #1 and #2 (in black) are set so that the resulting angle of the track is a 180 degree turn going either direction.

The example drawn in green illustrates placing Fence #2 above, or past the X axis, of Fence #1 creating an arc to the track that is approximately 270 degrees from Fence #1 (assuming you jump them from the right lead in the direction shown).

ᐱ The black Fences #1 and #2 are set so the resulting angle of the track is a 180-degree turn going either direction. The green example illustrates placing Fence #2 on a diagonal as opposed to a straight across. This results in a 270-degree angle between the two obstacles, allowing for a wider, more swooping turn (assuming you jump them from the right lead in the direction shown).

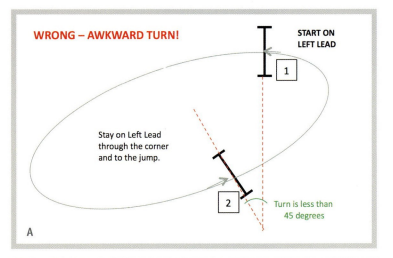

WRONG – AWKWARD TURN!

START ON LEFT LEAD

1

Stay on Left Lead through the corner and to the jump.

2

Turn is less than 45 degrees

A

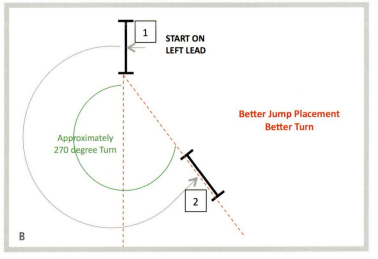

1

START ON LEFT LEAD

Better Jump Placement Better Turn

Approximately 270 degree Turn

2

B

ᐱ When fences are set at too close an angle (less than 90 degrees) as shown in A, it is almost impossible for the horse to make a smooth turn, even though both fences can be jumped off the left lead. An elliptical turn like this would never be used on a course in competition. By simply moving Fence #1 as shown in B, the two fences are now at an angle that is greater than 180 degrees (about 270 degrees). This ensures a much smoother turn.

lar to its center, which is best, as we have discussed), and keep the flow of the course much smoother. In order to determine the angle between two jumps, visualize a line extending straight out from the poles of each obstacle, creating a virtual angle that you can then measure (see illustration).

Bending Lines, Broken Lines, and Turning Out of a Line
Bending lines and *broken lines* follow a curved track between fences; the difference between them is that a *bending* line follows an arc that allows the horse to stay on the same lead between fences, while a *broken* line causes a change of direction—and a change of lead—between fences. Both are best for more experienced horses and riders, although even then they should feature at least six strides to allow for room for correction as necessary. Bending and broken lines are considered more technical because it is much harder to "see" the track and bend the horse correctly.

Creating a track that involves *turning out of a line* (in this case, meaning a *straight* line—see p. 15), is considered quite technical. You might see this question in upper-level equitation and jumper courses. However, it is not something I would routinely practice at home, even with a seasoned horse. And note, you should never ever design a course with a turn out of a *combination*—that is, a series of fences with a

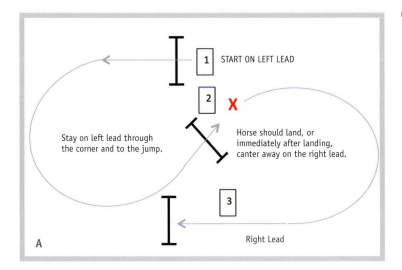

A

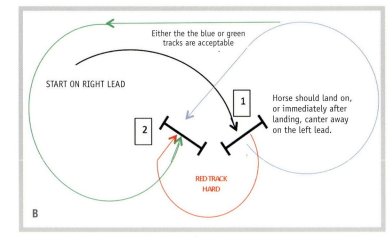

B

In A you can see examples of changing direction via a diagonal fence, going from the left lead to the right lead. This is a typical half-turn change of direction (see p. 18). In B, you start on the right lead (black) and change to the left over Fence #1. The blue "figure eight" track has almost a 360-degree turn. Either the blue or green tracks are acceptable for approaching Fence #2. You would not follow the red track (a reverse turn) unless you had a large enough space to allow for a long approach to the second fence.

> Although both of the drawings on this page have a sharply angled turn depicting a broken line, they demonstrate how where the apex of the turn is located can make such a line successful or not. In A the proposed turn is acceptable because the distance from Fence #1 to the apex of the turn is shorter than the distance from the apex to Fence #2, allowing the rider plenty of time to straighten and prepare for Fence #2. Although the drawing in B does not depict an illegal turn, per se, it would be very difficult to change leads, turn, and then jump the second fence in good form.

> It is not generally recommended to bend out of a line (red) but bending into a line (blue) is more common.

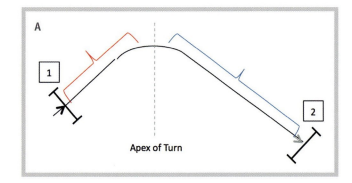

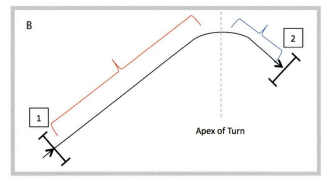

distance of fewer than three strides. Combinations are considered *one element* of a course, and you don't want your horse to ever consider running out of a distance set that short.

It is acceptable, however, to *turn back* or *bend into* a straight line. In such a case, the track becomes a pretty typical bending line. You can make a bending line easier by making the angle or the track between the two jumps almost straight. If you plan to set an option for bending into a straight line, make sure that the regular (straight)

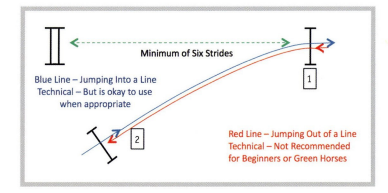

line is at least six strides long so the rider has time to make it clear to the horse where he is going.

The Trick with Angles

You want to avoid awkward angles in course design. As mentioned on the previous pages, the angle between two fences (when they are not in a straight line) should be 180 degrees or greater when building courses for general use and a variety of horse and rider levels.

In some cases, of course, you might want to set jumps at a sharper angle, perhaps as sharp as 90 degrees, such as when performing an "S" turn in an equitation class (basically a combination of two 90-degree turns). You also might set tighter angles when practicing sharper turns to shave off time in a jump-off. Be aware that the difficulty when jumping tightly angled fences is increased when you also have shorter distances between the fences. When using sharp angles, plan to allow enough room between the fences so they can be negotiated smoothly and safely.

QUICK REFERENCE:
NINE CONSIDERATIONS WHEN
DESIGNING A JUMP COURSE

1 Design your track first with consideration of the following qualities: The course should have a flowing track (allowing for a good pace and even rhythm), even if it has a high level of technicality and/or difficulty, and regardless of whether it is intended for the hunter, equitation, or jumper ring. The track should consist of straight lines and curved lines that are limited by the space you have available to you and the skill level of the horse and rider expected to negotiate it (see more about difficulty on p. 37).

2 Sketch out the skills you plan to work on and design your track accordingly, based upon the space and jump components available to you. (Note that when designing one of many courses that will be used in a day, you should consider where you put the track, your first fence, single fences, and related distances in the courses that will follow so that you keep repetition to a minimum and give the arena footing a rest.)

3 After you have a general idea of how your track will flow around the arena and you have an idea of what specific tests you want to include on your course, you can decide where you want to place your fences upon the

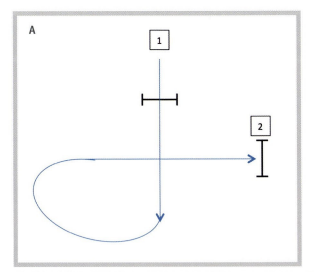

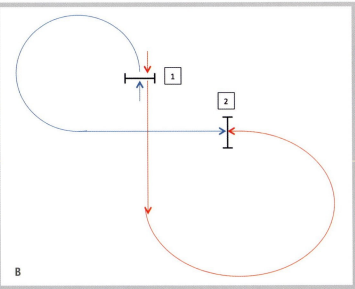

◀ In A you see one kind of *reverse turn*, where the rider turns away from the second fence in order to change direction in preparation to jumping it. In some cases, if you make a turn like this in competition with your back facing away from the fence you are traveling toward (in essence going right to turn left), it is considered a refusal or even an elimination. It is not a turn I recommend using in your schooling course design. In B you can see two different tracks with acceptable turns from Fence #1 to Fence #2.

V Setting fences with angles between them of less than 90 degrees such as shown by the red fence (the blue lines show the position of 90 degrees) creates a very technical question, a line that is impossible to ride, or a track that is just plain dangerous. The red fence is on a 45-degree angle to the two black fences. Notice how awkward this would make your track, regardless the direction of travel or the distance between the fences.

45-degree angle

track. Your fences should be numbered in the order in which they are to be jumped. Combinations (jumps with a related distance of three or fewer strides between them) are notated with a number. In the *hunter ring*, all fences are numbered consecutively, regardless of whether they are part of a line or part of a combination. The elements in a combination in the *jumper ring* are identified with the same number plus a letter indicating the order (for example, 1a, 1b, 1c). *Equitation fences* may be numbered as they are for the jumper ring, but you may also see them numbered consecutively, as in the hunter ring.

4 Your course needs at least one single fence that can be jumped off either lead, or two single fences, one of which is to be jumped off the right lead and one off the left.

5 Include at least one change of direction on your course. It can be through a single fence set on the diagonal, a diagonal line, a combination, or through roll-backs. Although it usually means that you need to set up more jumps, when schooling

you will probably prefer to have at least two changes in direction in your course so that you can practice changing onto either lead.

6 Aim to have half the jumps ridden on one lead and half on the other. When this isn't possible, plan to leave the course in place for a week and change the direction of some of the fences mid-week. Or, place ground lines on both sides of the fences so that they can be jumped from either direction at any time.

7 Design your course so that about half the fences are verticals and half are spreads.

8 Determine the approximate striding/distances between related fences (see more about distances beginning on p. 21). I initially draw related distances between fences, assuming a standard 12-foot stride. Then I adjust the distances so they are appropriate to the specific conditions when I physically set the course in the arena. Distances should always be adjusted as necessary for the horse and rider schooling them.

9 At this point you can translate your thoughts and sketches into a scale drawing of your proposed course (see the next chapter).

4

DRAWING
JUMP COURSES

- **Introduction to Drawing Jump Courses to Scale**
- **Easy Steps for Drawing a Jump Course Diagram**
- **Additional Setup Instructions**

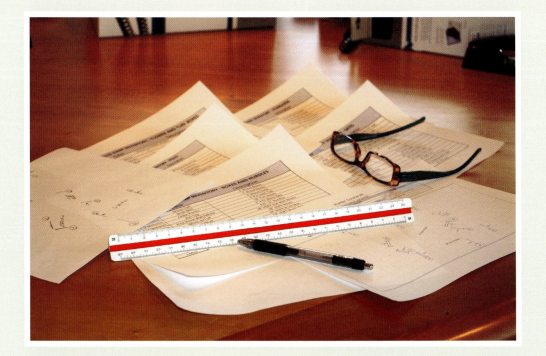

INTRODUCTION TO DRAWING JUMP COURSES TO SCALE

Drawing your course to scale is a necessary step before you move to the arena to set the course. Having a scale drawing in hand eliminates guesswork and having to move jump components numerous times. Your drawing must first reflect the exact dimensions of your arena; then everything should be clearly marked and/or described so that other individuals can "read" it. There are many software programs that can assist in drawing your course on your computer; however, for setting

schooling courses at home or at your barn, it is completely acceptable to hand-draw them on simple graph paper, as long as you keep the drawing to scale.

An engineering or architectural scale (ruler), a protractor, and graph paper are useful if you are drawing by hand. I use Microsoft PowerPoint, and find it relatively easy to draw the courses on the screen to scale, and cut and paste like components. Diagonal and bending lines are a little tricky to draw on the screen and I always check the distances with a scale (ruler) on a hard copy before considering them final.

For schooling purposes, it is completely acceptable to hand-draw jump course diagrams on simple graph paper, as long as you keep the drawing to scale.

EASY STEPS FOR DRAWING A JUMP COURSE DIAGRAM

1 Prepare an inventory of all of the jump components you have to work with, creating an up-to-date list of "available materials." This will include standards, gates, hurdles, boxes, poles, flowers, and other fill. Make sure you notate how many of each you have, what colors you have, and other details. This way you know what type of "furniture pieces" you have to "furnish" your course. (For suggestions on types of "furniture" to use, see p. 53.)

2 Create an accurate, to-scale drawing of the arena in which the jump course will be set. For my drawings I use .5 inch to equal 10 feet.

3 With the rough sketch showing the outline of your track in hand (you created this in the last chapter—see p. 38), mark the spots within your arena where jumps will be placed. You can use simple symbols to depict each jump (see the samples below).

4 Remember to consider space and distances. Draw the related distances between fences assuming a standard 12-foot stride. (As I've mentioned, when you actually set the course, or as different horses and students school over the fences, the distances between the related fences can be adjusted. See more about distance beginning on p. 21.)

5 When the arena has a fence or wall enclosing the perimeter, you need to accommodate adequate

> Common symbols to use in creating your course diagram.

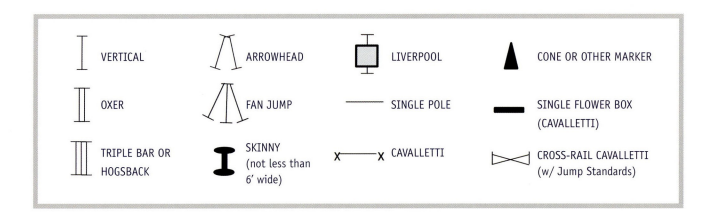

VERTICAL	ARROWHEAD	LIVERPOOL	CONE OR OTHER MARKER
OXER	FAN JUMP	SINGLE POLE	SINGLE FLOWER BOX (CAVALLETTI)
TRIPLE BAR OR HOGSBACK	SKINNY (not less than 6' wide)	CAVALLETTI	CROSS-RAIL CAVALLETTI (w/ Jump Standards)

STANDARDS		
Quantity	**Color**	**Description**
WING STANDARDS		
10 (5 pairs)	White	5' Wood Wing Standards
4 (2 pair)	Dark Green/White	5' Wood Wing Standards
4 (2 pair)	Brown	5' Wood Wing Standards
SCHOOLING (POST) STANDARDS		
10 (5 pair)	White	PVC Schooling Standards
4 (2 pair)	Green	PPL Schooling Standards
4 (2 pair)	Brown	PPL Schooling Standards
OTHER (DECORATIVE) STANDARDS		
2 (1 pair)	Cedar Trees	5' Cedar Trees
6 (3 pair)	Wood	6' Wood Fence Post Standards
GATES		
Quantity	**Color**	**Description**
2	White	Small White Solid w/"X"Gates (11" high)
2	Green	Small HDPE Gates (11" high)
2	Brown	Small HDPE Gates (11" high)
BOXES AND HURDLES		
Quantity	**Color**	**Description**
1 (2 Sections)	Brick Wall	2' Wood Boxes
1 (2 Sections)	Cedar	2' Wood Coop
1 (2 Sections)	Roll Top	2' PVC Roll Top
POLES		
Quantity	**Color**	**Description**
16	White	10' Painted Wood Poles
8	Dark Brown Varnish	10' Wood Poles
8	Green	10' Painted Wood Poles
8	Red	10' Painted Wood Poles

◄ Creating a list of available materials (every item available to you for building a course and constructing jumps) and keeping it up-to-date helps you plan and draw different courses on a regular basis.

> At a show, you would not see a description of each jump on the course diagram as I've included here. However, typing or writing them right on your diagram provides easy-to-use guidelines and directions for you and others when setting courses for schooling purposes.

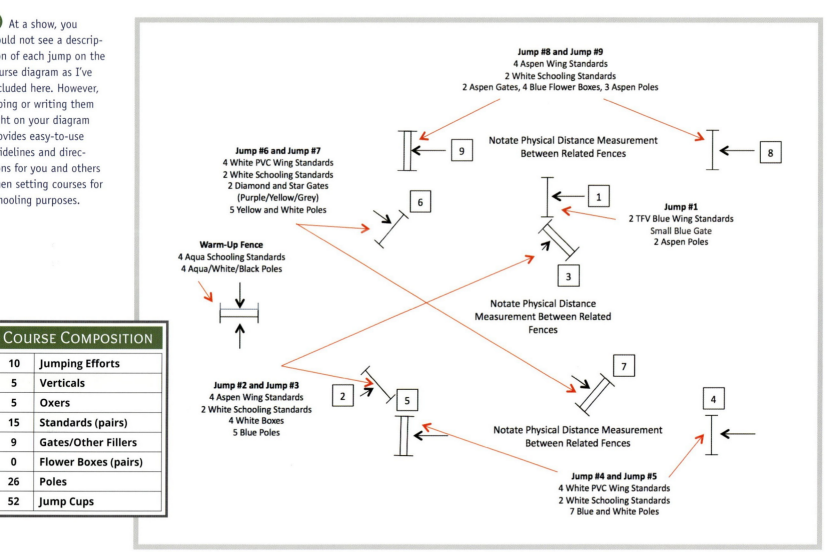

Jump #8 and Jump #9
4 Aspen Wing Standards
2 White Schooling Standards
2 Aspen Gates, 4 Blue Flower Boxes, 3 Aspen Poles

9

Notate Physical Distance Measurement
Between Related Fences

8

Jump #6 and Jump #7
4 White PVC Wing Standards
2 White Schooling Standards
2 Diamond and Star Gates
(Purple/Yellow/Grey)
5 Yellow and White Poles

6

1

Jump #1
2 TFV Blue Wing Standards
Small Blue Gate
2 Aspen Poles

Warm-Up Fence
4 Aqua Schooling Standards
4 Aqua/White/Black Poles

3

Notate Physical Distance
Measurement Between Related
Fences

7

Jump #2 and Jump #3
4 Aspen Wing Standards
2 White Schooling Standards
4 White Boxes
5 Blue Poles

2

5

4

Notate Physical Distance Measurement
Between Related Fences

Jump #4 and Jump #5
4 White PVC Wing Standards
2 White Schooling Standards
7 Blue and White Poles

COURSE COMPOSITION

10	Jumping Efforts
5	Verticals
5	Oxers
15	Standards (pairs)
9	Gates/Other Fillers
0	Flower Boxes (pairs)
26	Poles
52	Jump Cups

space at the ends and sides of the arena to allow for a safe approach and departure for each fence. When the approach or departure to a jump is out of a corner or involves turning toward (into) the rail, leave space equal to a minimum of three straight strides before and after the jump. Also leave from 42 (when the line is down the

V I suggest preparing a detailed jump composition worksheet such as this to ensure you and others can easily recreate the jump course you created on paper in the arena. Organization such as this ensures your careful planning during the conception of your course results in a safe, attractive, flowing course that both horses and riders can enjoy.

JUMP COMPOSITION WORKSHEET: JUMP COURSE EXAMPLE

Jump #	Description	Standards	Gates/Boxes	Ground Line	Poles
1	Cedar Coop Vertical	Two White Wood Wings	Cedar Coop (Two Sections)	Two Natural Wood Flower Boxes with Greenery	One Natural Pole over Coop
2	Burgundy Lattice Gate Vertical	Two Burgundy Lattice Wings	Burgundy Lattice Gate	Two Burgundy Flower Boxes, White Flowers	One Burgundy Pole over Gate
3	Burgundy Lattice Gate Oxer	Two Burgundy Lattice Wings Two Burgundy Schooling Standards	Burgundy Lattice Gate	Two Burgundy Flower Boxes, White Flowers	One Burgundy Pole over Gate, One Burgundy Pole on Back Element
4	Birch Gate Vertical	Two Birch Wings	Birch Gate Small Green Boxes (Two Sections)	Two White Flower Boxes, Yellow Flowers	One Birch Pole over Birch Gate
5	Birch Gate Oxer	Two Birch Wings Two White Schooling Standards	Birch Gate Small Green Boxes (Two Sections)	Two White Flower Boxes, Yellow Flowers	One Birch Pole over Birch Gate, One Birch Pole on Back element
6	Stone Wall Gate Vertical	Two Stone Insert Wings	Stone Insert Gate	Two White Flower Boxes, Purple Flowers	One Grey Pole Over Stone Gate
7	Stone Wall Gate Oxer	Two Stone Insert Wings Two Grey Schooling Standards	Stone Insert Gate	Two White Flower Boxes, Purple Flowers	One Grey Pole Over Stone Gate, One Grey Pole on Back Element
8	Brick Wall Oxer	Two White Wood Wings Two White Schooling Standards	Brick Boxes (Two Sections) Small White Gate	Two White Flower Boxes, Red Flowers	One White pole Over Boxes One White Pole on Back Element

PULL SHEET FOR JUMP COURSE MATERIAL		
Quantity	**Color**	**Description**
STANDARDS		
4 (2 pair)	White	5' Wood Wing Standards
4 (2 pair)	Burgundy/Lattice	5' PVC Wing Standards
4 (2 pair)	Grey w/ Stone Inserts	5' HDPE Slant Wing Standards
4 (2 pair)	Aspen	5' HDPE Wing Standards
4 (2 pair)	White	5' PVC Schooling Stndards
2 (1 pair)	Burgundy	5' HDPE Schooling Standards
2 (1 pair)	Grey	5' HDPE Schooling Standards
GATES BOXES AND HURDLES		
1 (2 sections)	Cedar	Cedar Coops
1 (2 sections)	Brick	Wood Boxes
2	Burgundy/Lattice	24" PVC Lattice Gates
2	Grey w/ Stone Inset	24" HDPE Gates
2	White	18" HDPE Gates
2	Green	18" HDPE Boxes
1	White	11" HDPE Gate
1	Natural	10' Wood Pole
3	Grey	10' HDPE Wrapped Poles
3	Burgundy	10' HDPE Wrapped Poles
3	Aspen	10' HDPE Wrapped Poles
2	White	10' Wood Pole
10 (5pair)	White	HDPE Flower Boxes
2 (1 pair)	Natural Wood	Wood Flower Boxes
4 (2 pair)	Burgundy	HDPE Flower Boxes
40 (20 pair)	Black Metal	Jump Cups

long side of the arena) to 54 (when the line is diagonal across the arena) feet for each of the four corners of the arena. Your diagram needs to reflect adequate room to get to, and land from, all the jumps.

6 Double-check your turns and angles with a protractor to ensure safe and flowing circles, semicircles, and changes of direction, such as described in the previous chapter (see p. 44).

7 Notate on your course diagram, or on a separate sheet, the components (from your list of available materials) that will make up each fence. Include details, such as a simple descriptor or color for the standards, gates, poles, boxes, and flowers.

ADDITIONAL SETUP INSTRUCTIONS

After drawing the course diagram, I always complete two additional charts to aid my memory and help others in setting the course I have designed. The first is a *jump composition worksheet*, which describes what is needed to construct each individual jump (see p. 55). The second is a *pull sheet*, which is particularly useful

◀ Prepare a *pull sheet* after you have drawn your course and once you know the details for each jump. This inventory list aids in efficiency, ensuring you gather all and only the components that you need to set the course.

when jump components are stored away from the arena or off-site. This specifies all the materials you need to construct the course (see chart, p. 56). These two charts aid in efficiency; you may have others that you determine help you and others construct jump courses at your facility.

The charts and lists I have provided in this book assume that vertical fences use two poles when no other filler is used on the jump. When filler is used on a vertical, only one pole is needed.

For oxers, I assume three poles are used, two on the front element and one on the back element, unless filler is used. When there is filler, one pole is placed over the filler on the front element and one pole is placed on the back element.

Don't forget the basics! You need two jump cups for every pole and two jump cups for hanging filler. Ground lines need to be added to your pole count. While they are considered optional, they are highly recommended for beginners and green horses as they aid with depth perception.

5

SETTING
THE COURSE

- **How to Set and Build a Course**
- **Safety Considerations When Designing and Constructing a Course**
- **Decorating the Course: Ideas for Finishing Touches**
- **How to Walk Your Course**

HOW TO SET AND BUILD A COURSE

1 When you are setting a jump course with the help of others, review the *pull sheet*, the *jump composition worksheet*, and *course diagram* that you created in the last chapter with them prior to beginning.

2 Collect only the components you need for the course in question. Check everything as you collect it to make sure it is in good repair—look for broken or splintered pieces, loose bolts, warping or cracking. Fix or replace potentially unsafe items before using them on course.

3 Lay out all the poles for the course in the arena first— one pole for each vertical, two poles for each oxer, three poles for a triple, and so on. (It is much easier to move a single pole than a completed fence!) Lay the poles for the fences that will be along the outer perimeter of your course first, especially when the arena has a fence around it. You can then move the jumps inward toward the center of your arena or change the angle of the jumps to provide more room if necessary. (When you begin by setting the inside lines, you can get "stuck" in a situation where you don't have enough space because you can't move the arena edge or perimeter fence outward to

◭ When setting your course, begin by placing all the poles on course first, flat on the ground. Check your angles and distances against your diagram and make necessary adjustments. *Then* construct your jumps. It is much easier to move and adjust the placement of poles than entire jumps!

accommodate.) Be sure you leave enough room for take-offs and landings, and that there is adequate room for a tractor and drag to get around the jumps. Check angles and distances between obstacles with a tape measure.

4 Set up the standards next. Keep in mind space constraints and space-saving options. You will save substantial space in your arena if you use schooling standards that are roughly 12 inches wide rather than wing standards that are typically 3 feet wide. (When your space is limited, consider using shorter poles, too—it is perfectly

acceptable in schooling courses to use 8- to 10-foot poles.) Create a frame for each jump by placing the top pole in jump cups set at the approximate height on the standards. Using your tape measure, check the height of the fence from the ground to the top of the highest rail and adjust as necessary. When setting spread fences, measure the width of the jump from the center of the front rail to the center of the back rail.

5 Walk the distances between the "frames." Confirm there is no interference of track between the ele-

> Here you see a jumper course being reset between classes. Note how the yellow and white poles in the background on the left and the poles in the corner on the far right are "banked" against the wing standards and wall to get them out of the way of the drag.

ments and that you can take the track to each fence as you planned on paper.

6 Cross-measure all lines and combinations (see p. 40). Make sure all related obstacles are square before going any further. After you have "squared-up" your lines, double-check your angles and distances to be sure you didn't inadvertently alter any.

7 Consider the specific conditions in the arena and/ or the horses and riders that will be schooling the course in the day(s) ahead, and make any final adjustments to the track or angles of the jumps to accommodate them. Remember that even the best course designers sometimes have to make changes to their plan once they start to build the course and "see it in real life."

8 Once you are satisfied that the jumps are in the right place, add your fill, including gates, walls, planks, hurdles, and flower boxes. When additional ground lines are needed, this is the time to add those, as well.

> Pole-and-plank fences, such as these two examples, are suitable for many levels, attractive, and easy to move and adjust. Choosing to set verticals like these throughout the course is particularity important when your training program, or those of your fellow boarders, requires that both fence height and related distances are changed frequently to accommodate different horses, riders, and jumping disciplines.

9 Go through and check all your jump cups to ensure they are secured safely and correctly. When using those that attach to jump standards with pins, check that the pin goes all the way through the first hole on the cup, through the post of the standard, and then through the hole on the other side of the jump cup. When a pin is only pushed partially through the post, or not set through both sides of the jump cup, the pin will bend or break when the pole or other filler is hit hard.

10 Do one last course walk and make any final adjustments needed. (See p. 66 for instructions on how to correctly and effectively walk your course.)

SAFETY CONSIDERATIONS WHEN DESIGNING AND CONSTRUCTING A COURSE

When designing and then constructing a jump course, safety for both the horses and the riders who will be using it should be the priority. To promote good form, set jumps in an inviting way, and as I've mentioned already, consider safe angles for turns and changes of direction, and always allow plenty of room for the approach and landing. A ground line makes judging distances easier, so include one where appropriate. When the fence is to be jumped from both directions, there should be ground lines on both sides.

Consider color when you set your course—some components blend in while others stand out, and visibility can

> Note how the burgundy standards blend into the darker background/footing when used inside. White, striped, or lighter colored standard, poles, and fillers (such as the lattice gate) would make this jump much easier to see.

make a course more or less difficult for horse and rider to navigate it successfully.

Fences must be able to break away and fall cleanly when a horse hits it during his jump. When a fence is to be jumped from both directions, it should fall cleanly to either side. Gates and boxes should be topped by a pole so it is more likely the pole is rattled or knocked out of the cups than the whole jump torn down. There should be at least a hand's width between the hanging component and the jump standard when the end of a pole or gate is placed in the cup. This allows it to fall more easily when a horse hits it. Gates should never be leaned into the standards in order to reduce their height as they can easily become wedged in the jump cups and will not fall easily when they are hit. Jump cups and jump components (including standards) should be in good repair and should not have sharp edges or elements that could scratch, puncture, trap, or otherwise harm horse or rider.

It is recommended that jump cups not be left on the standards when they are "empty" (a pole or gate is not in them). However, when they are removed they should be set aside in a designated area—they should not be thrown on the ground in the vicinity of a jump where a horse could step on one or a tractor or drag could run it over. Gates and poles should also not be left lying in the footing. Gates, especially, are made to hang on cups, and leaving them lying on the ground or against the standards causes warping and/or twisting of the component.

MOVING JUMP COMPONENTS EFFICIENTLY AND SAFELY

Here are a few rules of thumb when setting and building a jump course:

- Wear sturdy shoes and gloves when moving jump components around your arena.

- Stand close to the object that you are moving.

- Center yourself and place your feet shoulder-width apart.

- Make sure you are standing straight in front of the component and that you are not twisting your body as you position yourself to lift it.

- Tighten your abdominal muscles as you bend your knees. Keep your knees over your feet and your feet flat on the ground. Your spine should be straight— most back injuries happen from bending forward when the back is rounded and bending from the waist rather than through the hips and knees.

- Make sure you have a good grasp on the component and hold it close to your body as you move it.

- Go slowly, and if the component is too heavy, get help.

V Stand close to the jump component (A), keep your back straight (B), and bend at the knees (C) when moving elements while setting and building your jump course.

• Follow the same rules listed above when you put the component down.

• *Never* drag jump components. It leaves ruts in the footing, and it is hard on the joints of the jump components and hard on your back.

DECORATING THE COURSE— IDEAS FOR FINISHING TOUCHES

Decorations on schooling courses are not just for purposes of "beautification." They have a training purpose in that they can be used to desensitize horses to the many unexpected things they may encounter at a horse show.

I encourage spending the extra time to add finishing touches, such as flowers, shrubs, and flags, because in the end you and your horse benefit from the "realistic" course scenario (not to mention the course looks nicer when left up for several days!)

It is important to use common sense when adding decorations to a jump course used for schooling purposes. Since schooling courses are often set up for significantly longer periods of time than those built for a horse show, decorative elements have to be able to stand up to the weather and the wind—at least when in an outdoor arena. They should be firmly secured to avoid a loose and flapping (and therefore, scary) appearance. Again, keep safety in mind when adding decoration—nothing should have a sharp edge that could cut either a horse or rider. And, like poles, fill, and standards, they need to be set so they fall out of the way, or with the poles or standards, when they are hit by either a horse or rider.

Artificial flowers, shrubs, and trees add color and make fences more inviting. Although you do not typically see flower boxes as ground lines in jumper classes as you do in the hunters, it is common for jumper fences to have small flower boxes or shrubs placed between the feet of the wing standards. In addition, such flower boxes can be weighted to give some additional stability to the wing standards.

It is quite common in every jumping discipline to add shrubs and trees in front of wing standards or slightly off to the side of a jump. Potted flowers can be placed on top of pillars (when they are used in lieu of wing standards) and standards can be (safely) rigged to accommodate hanging flower baskets. At shows, decorative elements are usually added to both front and back sides of the fence, most likely for photographic purposes, as jumping pictures are often taken from the back side as the horse is jumping toward the camera.

Hay or straw bales can be easily found and implemented as decoration on your course. They are commonly used as filler for jumps in hunter or equitation classes. Garlands are another good choice to weave through your standards or brush box, rather than real branches. Just make sure they are securely attached or weighted in a manner that will not interfere with the ability to adjust the height of the fence.

Artificial rocks can be used in lieu of cones to mark *focal points*—specific objects or points in the distance for riders to focus on as their horse goes over the fence—and can be grouped together to make an island or laid out in a line to make a small jump.

Waving flags and banners hung from the perimeter fence—such as those seen at a horse show—can be especially distracting to a horse when he hasn't seen such things before. If you have flags and banners to use when you set your course, add some in strategic places. But you can achieve the desired desensitization by simply hanging a couple of jackets or coolers on the arena

fence. Acquainting your horse with such "surprises" in schooling makes it easier for him to ignore them when you get to a horse show.

HOW TO WALK YOUR COURSE

One of the benefits of designing and building your own jump courses is having the opportunity to walk them. Perfecting your course walk can go a long way to improving your round. Walking and rewalking lines as you determine that the distances are set correctly can help you cultivate an eye for finding the right takeoff spot.

Even before stepping foot on your course, practice walking in 3-foot (1-yard) increments (you'll need this ability when planning distances, such as discussed earlier in this book—see p. 21). When you can consistently take 3-foot steps, it is relatively easy to determine a horse's 12-foot stride. As mentioned, one horse stride is equal to four human steps (12 feet/4 yards).

1 You begin walking a line from the back of the first fence in the line. Your back and heels should touch the back of the first fence before you start striding and counting your 3-foot steps.

2 Walk forward and count the number of 3-foot steps it takes to reach the front of the next fence. Count your 3-foot steps in sets of four—ONE-2-3-4, TWO-2-3-4, THREE-2-3-4, FOUR-2-3-4, and so on—until you arrive at the base of the next jump. The number of strides in the line is *one less* than the total sets of four counted because you have to allow 6 feet for landing and 6 feet for takeoff (a total of 12 feet or one stride). For example, if you take 20 3-foot steps, the distance between the fences is 60 feet, or five strides, minus one for landing and takeoff—so a "normal" four-stride line.

3 Follow the track and proceed to the next fence, and the next, noting turns and related distances as you go.

COURSE-WALKING LINGO

What does the term "normal" mean when used in conjunction with a distance? When the distance from one fence to another can be counted in a complete set of four, 3-foot steps, it is considered a "normal" distance because it correlates with a 12-foot stride.

When the distance is one step *less than* a complete set of four 3-foot steps, then the line is slightly "short" and shorter, steady strides are needed to ride it accurately. When the distance is one step *more than* a complete set of four 3-foot steps, then the line is slightly "long" and more pace and forward motion is required.

When the distance is two steps off from a complete set of four 3-foot steps, it is on the "half-stride" and the rider must decide whether to extend the horse to ride a

Riders walk the course with their trainers prior to the start of an International Hunter Derby Class.

very forward line in the least number of strides, or to collect the horse, shorten his normal stride, and add an extra stride between fences.

HOW THE COURSE WILL RIDE

When you first walk your complete course after setting it, adjust any really difficult distances and walk it again. When creating courses for more advanced horses and riders, you can set lines short or long, although it should be noted that for different horses, and due to various external factors, lines will ride differently anyway.

For example, ground conditions can influence distances to fences. Declines and inclines change the strid-

ing: a line sloping downhill will tend to ride slightly shorter than the same line from the opposite direction. Good footing tends to make distances ride "true," while soft, deep footing or excessively hard footing may affect pace and stride length and make distances ride longer. Walking the course allows you to pay attention to the footing on landings, takeoffs, and the condition of the tracks of rollbacks and tight turns. Pay particular attention to how multiple landings from many horses may affect the footing.

When footing is of particular concern, as the designer of the course, it may be in the best interests of all who will use the course to make modifications that allow for a revised track and a safer ride for everyone.

6

Grids, Gymnastics, and Mini-Courses

for Small Arenas and Limited Jump Inventories

Theoretically, as long as the horse's body is straight on approach, in the air, and upon landing, he should be able to jump an obstacle from either lead and either direction, and thus "clear" a course. But jump courses also require you and your horse ride on the flat *between* fences, ride both straight lines and curves, and to alternate between these in order to make the entire round flow.

The truth is, you actually spend more time moving *around* the course than you spend jumping obstacles, so you really don't need a lot of jumps to school your horse—you just need to properly use the ones you have. If you have a regular instructor or trainer, he or she may take a different approach, but I rarely work with more than four obstacles in any one session. Some of my hardest lessons have been with only one or two fences, concentrating on one or two skills. With this in mind, most of the sample courses provided in this section are "classic" exercises and, as my trainer frequently states, "simple but not necessarily easy."

Please note that the courses in this section are **not** drawn to scale. The exact placement for your fences and the distances between related obstacles depends upon the size of the arena in which you ride. You will likely set your lines at four to five strides (six if your arena is long enough). For those with a "narrow" arena (less than 75

An example of a gymnastic grid: trot to a bounce to a two-stride oxer.

feet), know that you are limited as to what you can safely do across the middle, and you may not have the physical space to complete all of the exercises in this section. If you are not sure whether the arena can safely accommodate one or more of the exercises, consult your trainer or instructor.

As with any course set for schooling purposes, the simpler the components used in grids, gymnastics, and mini courses, the easier they are to move around. Schooling standards, poles, planks, and small gates are the easiest to adjust and will offer you the most versatility.

GRIDS AND GYMNASTIC EXERCISES

Grids are a kind of *gymnastic exercise* for horses. They emphasize straightness, rhythm, and the ability to adjust the horse's stride. They are often used to perfect a horse's jumping form or the rider's position over fences. Eventually, a solid foundation of grid work can lead to mastering the technical combinations that you see in higher-level hunter, equitation, and jumper courses.

Grids have their own set of generally accepted distances for the elements contained within them. Because most grids use three or fewer strides between ele-

◀ Using simple jump components, such as poles, schooling standards, and basic gates as shown in these indoor and outdoor examples, make it easier to move and adjust grids during a schooling session.

ments, setting appropriate distances for the exercises is extremely important.

SAFE GRID PROGRESSION

When you work with a grid, start with only one or two elements and build up from there. When you are riding, a ground person is necessary to help ensure the correct distances and adjust the fence height. Because of the fewer number of strides between elements, more accuracy is required than when riding longer lines. Appropriate distances depend on the number of strides between elements and the gait used in approaching the grid.

A grid should be introduced with ground poles, progressing to cross-rails, and then to verticals and/or spreads. Grids are typically built using poles only, although a small flower box as fill or as a ground line, or a small gate to give more depth to the grid, is completely appropriate. As mentioned, using fewer and simpler components makes it easier to tear down and rebuild the grid as you progress through your riding session or ride different horses.

Since gymnastic exercises work on one or two skills at a time, they can become boring for both horse and rider when they are repeated over and over. Also, because gymnastic exercises are designed to build physical strength and body awareness in both horse and rider, they can quickly become physically and mentally exhausting. Change the exercise frequently in order to keep repetition to a minimum.

DISTANCE CHART FOR POLES USED IN GYMNASTICS AND GRIDS

Trot Poles	4' - 4'6" Apart
Canter Poles	8' - 10' Apart
Placing Pole in Front of Jump Approaching from a Trot	7' - 9'
Placing Pole in Front, or on Backside, of Jump Approaching from a Canter	8'6" - 10'

Basic recommended distances for ground poles used in gymnastics and grids, adapted from the *USHJA Trainer Certification Manual*.

DISTANCE CHART FOR ELEMENTS IN GYMNASTICS AND GRIDS

	Approaching First Element in Grid From Trot	Approaching First Element in Grid From Canter	Competition Distance at a "Normal" 12' Stride
Bounce No-Stride	9'6" - 10'6"	10' - 11'6"	11'6" - 12
1 Stride	18' - 20'	19' - 22'	24' - 25'
2 Stride	28' - 30'	30' - 33'	35' - 36'
3 Stride	39' - 43'	41' - 45'	48'
4 Stride	50' - 55'	52' - 57'	60'
5 Stride	61' - 67'	63' - 68'	72'

Basic recommended distances between elements in gymnastics and grids, adapted from the *USHJA Trainer Certification Manual*.

Crids and Gymnastic Exercises

The following grids and gymnastic exercises can be inserted into lessons as needed and used as warm-ups or refreshers for basic skills that will be called upon later in a lesson. Most gymnastics are set low (often just poles on the ground or cross-rails), and for most riders, they shouldn't exceed 3 to 3 1/2 feet. They are not generally used to improve "scope" (the ability to jump higher/wider obstacles) but are more often used to polish form (both horse and rider) and practice rhythm and pace. As mentioned, the nature of gymnastic exercises makes them physically (and mentally) challenging—keeping the height low allows the horse to practice more without being overly taxing on joints and soft tissues.

Gymnastic exercises are used to isolate, practice, and perfect a specific skill before riding an entire course. Gymnastic exercises are similar to breaking down individual dance steps when choreographing an entire performance.

Note: The diagrams in this chapter were created with a vertical orientation (see p. 39). Square and rectangular outlines in these diagrams do not accurately represent the arena boundary. When setting the exercises in this section, make sure there is room for a safe approach to and landing from each fence, as well as space for turns between obstacles and the fence line or wall.

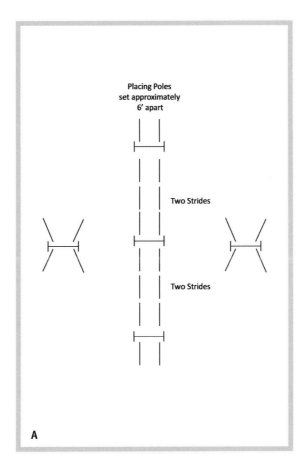

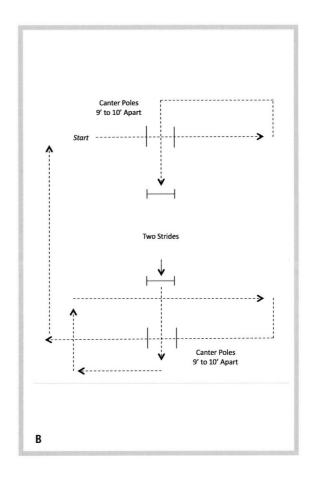

PLACING POLES FOR STRAIGHTNESS A & B

NOTES: These two exercises, using *placing poles* to help develop straightness in the horse, can be done at a trot or canter. The exercise in B uses reverse turns, which you may remember are "technically" illegal (see p. 48), but have uses in schooling scenarios. If you have trouble with flying lead changes, do simple lead changes instead.

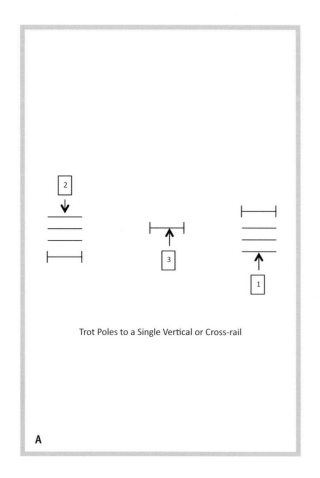

Trot Poles to a Single Vertical or Cross-rail

A

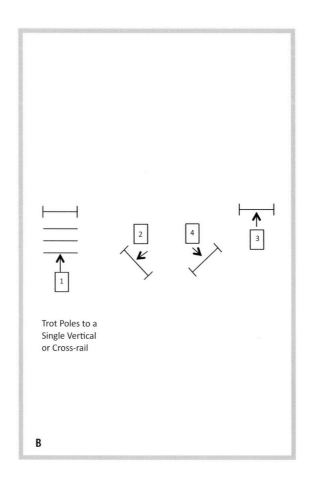

Trot Poles to a
Single Vertical
or Cross-rail

B

GRID EXERCISES 1 A & B

NOTES: These grid exercises work on steering and rhythm by introducing a single jump, with and without trot poles.
In Exercise B, practice going deep into the corners of your arena after Fence #2 and #4.

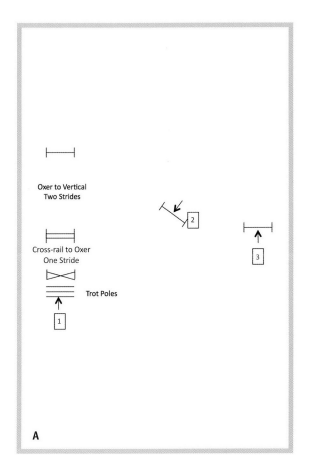

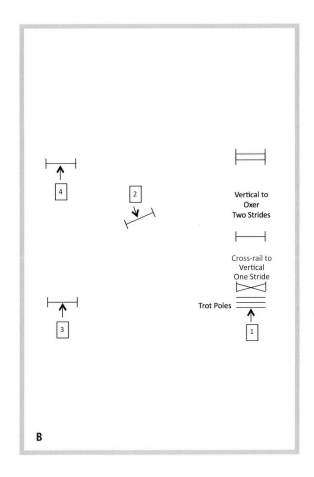

GRID EXERCISES 2 A & B

NOTES: Two exercises with a trot into the grid and canter out feature. Beginners should stick with cross-rails and simple vertical fences where oxers are noted in the diagrams. These grid exercises are especially useful for improving the rider's position and strength.

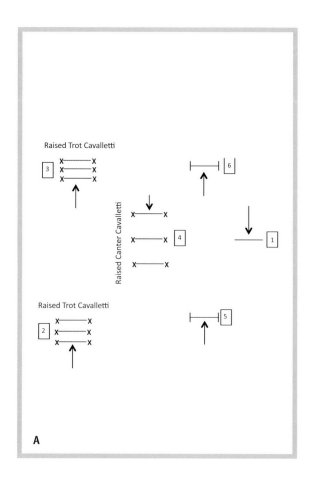

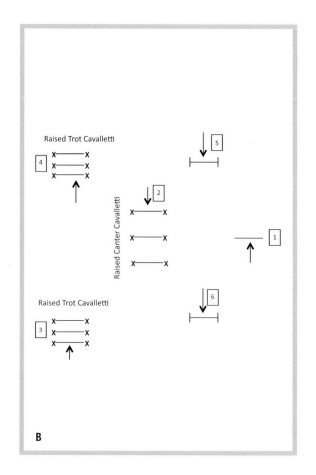

GRID EXERCISES 3 A & B

NOTES: Serpentine exercises are about rhythm, changing the horse's bend from one side to the other (flexibility), and steering. These two variations on a short-loop serpentine use poles, raised cavalletti, and low jumps.

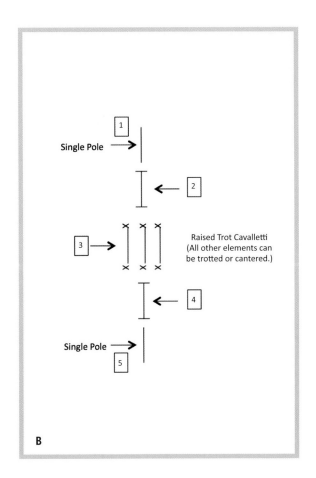

GRID EXERCISES 4 A & B

NOTES: These two variations on a four-loop serpentine use poles, cavalletti, and low jumps. Both of these exercises are for practicing lateral flexibility. Note that in Exercise A you turn left after Single Pole #3 to loop around and weave back down the other way to Fence #4. Exercise B has tighter turns (serpentine loops) so it is harder to execute than Exercise A.

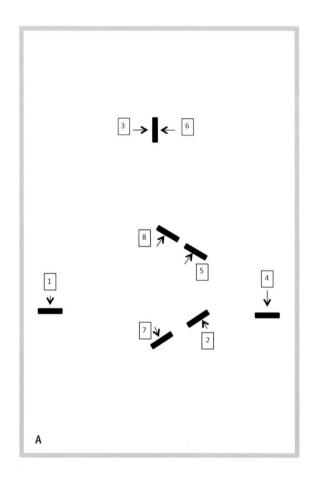

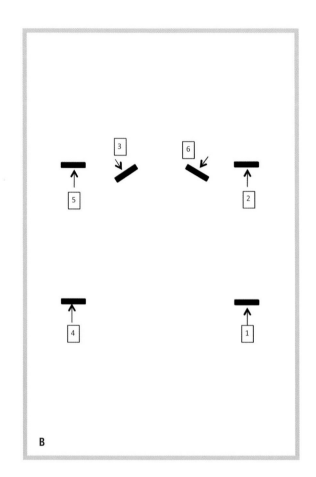

STEERING EXERCISES 1 A & B

NOTES: These gymnastic exercises use narrow flower boxes (approximately 3½ to 4 feet in width) to practice steering and accuracy. You can substitute short poles, small cavalletti, or cross-rails. Exercise A provides a visual template for the rider to learn to go deep into corners before and after each flower box. In A, travel around Box #2 and #7 when traveling from #4 to #5. In Exercise B, Box #3 and #6 are for practicing a short approach to a jump when turning out of a corner.

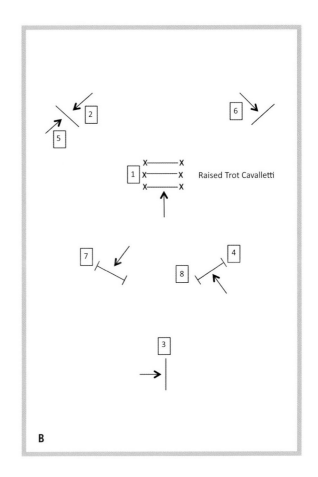

STEERING EXERCISES 2 A & B

NOTES: These two exercises should only use poles, small cavalletti, and cross-rails. Their emphasis is on steering and riding deep into the corners. You can perform these at a trot or at a canter with simple lead changes. These exercises are similar to those on p. 77—Exercise B is in a figure-eight pattern, and the poles are set to encourage the rider to use the entire arena.

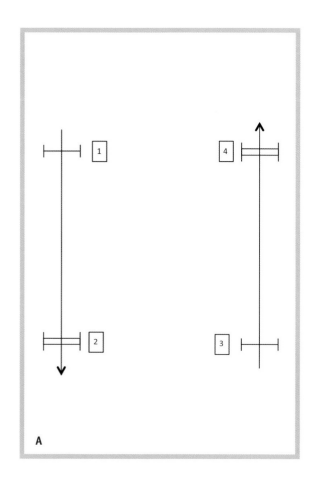

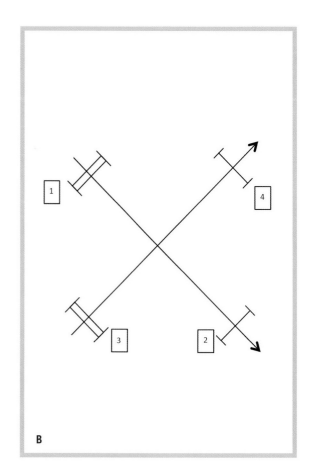

LINES 1 A & B

NOTES: Here, two scenarios provide practice riding vertical to oxer lines, and oxer to vertical lines. These exercises emphasize riding straight lines on either straight or diagonal tracks. Use simple jump components so it is easy to alter the lines for various distances.

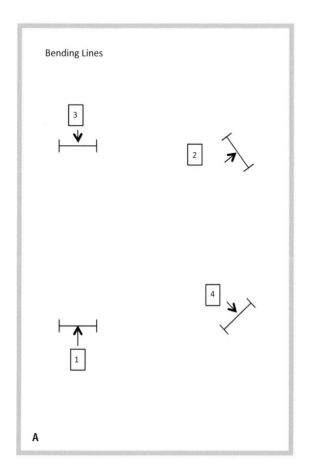

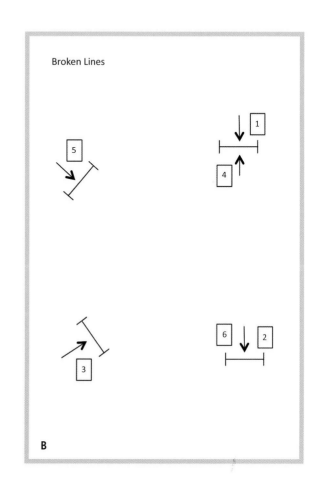

LINES 2 A & B

NOTES: These two exercises help you practice bending or broken lines. Alter the setups shown here to fit your arena, and remember that it is recommended you have six or more strides between obstacles on these kinds of lines. Bending and broken lines are "technical," and should only be used by horses and riders who have the appropriate skill level and experience. In Exercise A, start on the right lead and stay on the right lead until you land after Fence #2; Fence #3 and #4 should be jumped from the left lead. In Exercise B, start on the right lead and change to the left lead just before Fence #4, and back to the right before Fence #6.

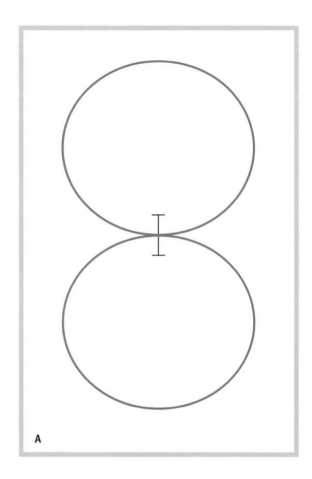

A

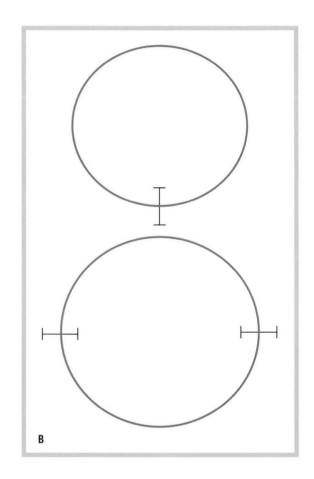

B

CIRCLE EXERCISES 1 A & B

NOTES: If your ring is extremely narrow (see p. 69), you may not be able to set these exercises. You need enough room for a comfortable turn through the middle. Practice beginning on both left and right leads. These are harder than they look and the more fences included on your circles, the harder they become. In A, you can circle on one lead over the pole or small jump, then stop and change directions, repeating the exercise on the opposite lead. You can also ride it as a figure eight, performing a lead change over the obstacle. Exercise B is about maintaining rhythm and bend, from the single jump on one circle, to two jumps on the second circle. Both exercises teach you to focus on pace and track.

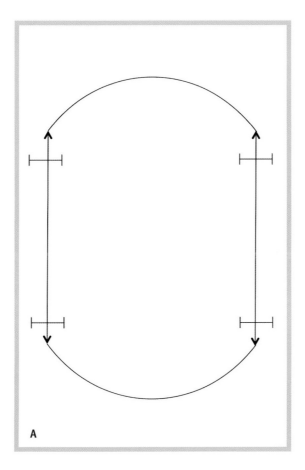

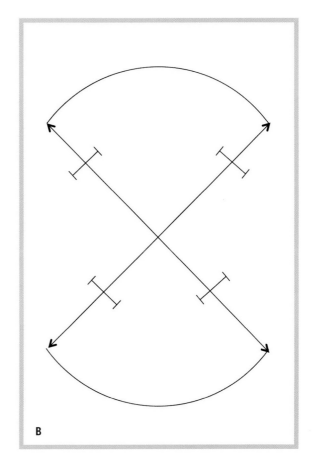

CIRCLE EXERCISES 2 A & B

NOTES: These variations on the circle exercise allow you to focus on maintaining your canter rhythm when coming out of a corner and then keeping your track straight through a line. Use all the space available to you when you make your turns at the end of the arena. Again, practice on both leads. Set the fences with ground lines on both sides so that you can jump them from either direction.

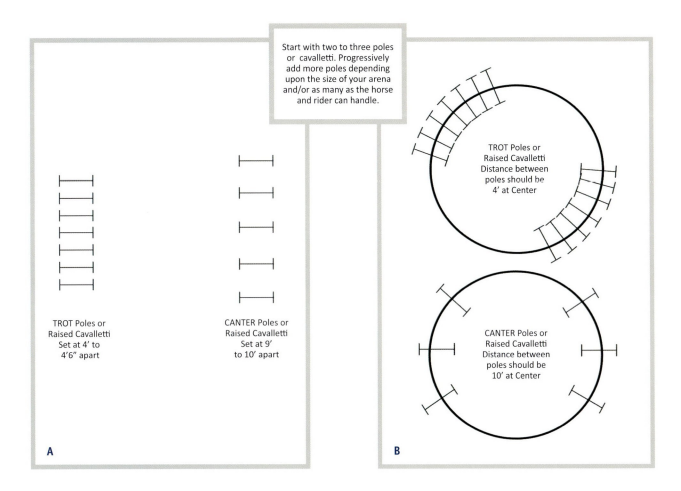

Start with two to three poles or cavalletti. Progressively add more poles depending upon the size of your arena and/or as many as the horse and rider can handle.

TROT Poles or Raised Cavalletti Distance between poles should be 4' at Center

CANTER Poles or Raised Cavalletti Distance between poles should be 10' at Center

TROT Poles or Raised Cavalletti Set at 4' to 4'6" apart

CANTER Poles or Raised Cavalletti Set at 9' to 10' apart

A

B

RHYTHM EXERCISES 1 A & B

NOTES: Consistent rhythm, where each fence is met out of the same even stride length, is the hallmark of a beautiful hunter or equitation round. Practicing on a circle is a great way to learn to establish this all-important rhythm. These two exercises use poles or small cavalletti. Start with two or three poles or cavalletti and progressively add more, depending on the size of your arena and the number the horse and rider can handle. These exercises are tiring to both horse and rider, so don't over use them.

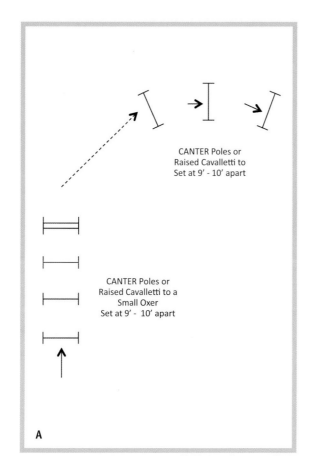

CANTER Poles or
Raised Cavalletti to
Set at 9' - 10' apart

CANTER Poles or
Raised Cavalletti to a
Small Oxer
Set at 9' - 10' apart

A

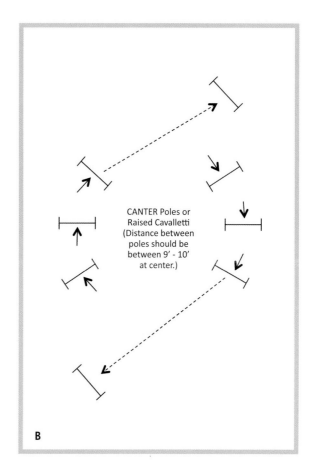

CANTER Poles or
Raised Cavalletti
(Distance between
poles should be
between 9' - 10'
at center.)

B

RHYTHM EXERCISES 2 A & B

NOTES: The exercises in these two diagrams show small jumps, but they can also be effective using cavalletti or ground poles. The bending line, either to or from the canter poles, makes this exercise more difficult and not recommended for beginners.

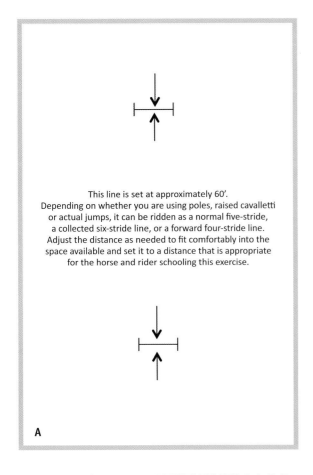

This line is set at approximately 60'.
Depending on whether you are using poles, raised cavalletti
or actual jumps, it can be ridden as a normal five-stride,
a collected six-stride line, or a forward four-stride line.
Adjust the distance as needed to fit comfortably into the
space available and set it to a distance that is appropriate
for the horse and rider schooling this exercise.

A

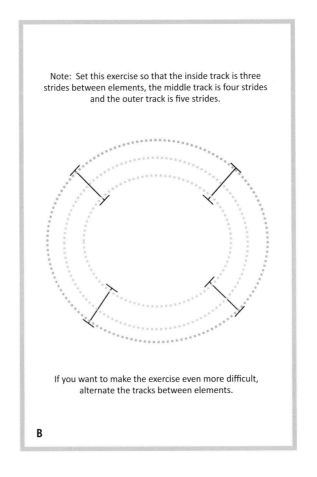

Note: Set this exercise so that the inside track is three
strides between elements, the middle track is four strides
and the outer track is five strides.

If you want to make the exercise even more difficult,
alternate the tracks between elements.

B

STRIDE LENGTH AND ADJUSTABILITY 1 A & B

NOTES: Jumpers need to be adjustable. On the left is a 60-foot line that can be practiced using either verticals or oxers in four forward, five normal, or six collected strides. The circle exercise in B is difficult and is used to create awareness of track and improve ability to keep the canter stride consistent. It should be practiced using ground poles or small vertical fences; the jumps should be set so they can be jumped from either direction.

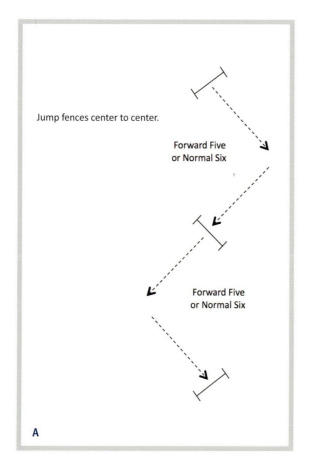

Jump fences center to center.

Forward Five
or Normal Six

Forward Five
or Normal Six

A

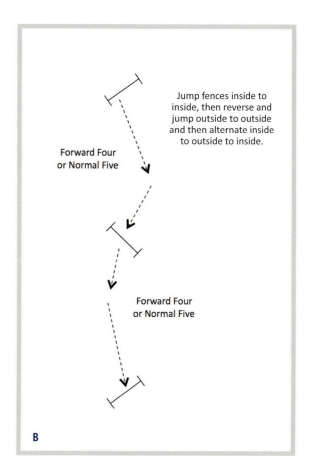

Jump fences inside to
inside, then reverse and
jump outside to outside
and then alternate inside
to outside to inside.

Forward Four
or Normal Five

Forward Four
or Normal Five

B

STRIDE LENGTH AND ADJUSTABILITY 2 A & B

NOTES: In a jumper class, the fences can come up quickly, and the rider needs to be prepared to adjust the horse's stride and bend as needed. This is especially important when the goal is to "shave off" time in a jump-off. The rider needs to be looking up and thinking ahead for the next obstacle. The tighter the distance between these fences, the harder these two exercises will be. They should only be used by horses and riders who can adjust their stride and are comfortable "seeing a distance."

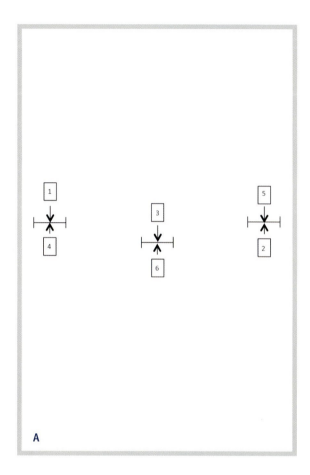

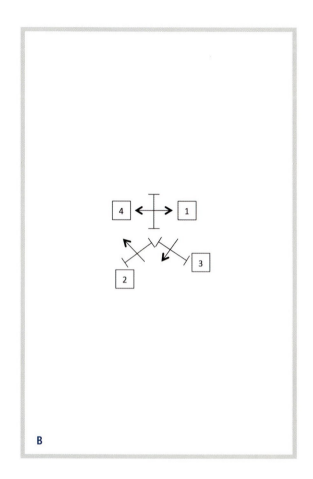

ROLLBACKS 1 A & B

NOTES: Equitation classes almost always have a test that includes a rollback. You should set the fences in these two fairly advanced exercises so that they can be jumped in either direction and off either lead. Make sure that you have adequate room between the fences and the rail to be able to complete smooth turns. Your ring should be at least 100-feet wide to set the exercise in A and keep your turns smooth. Exercise A is a more advanced version of the serpentines on p. 75. The angled fences in B make it a more useful exercise when your ring is narrow. This is a fun track to change and see how many different ways you can jump these three fences.

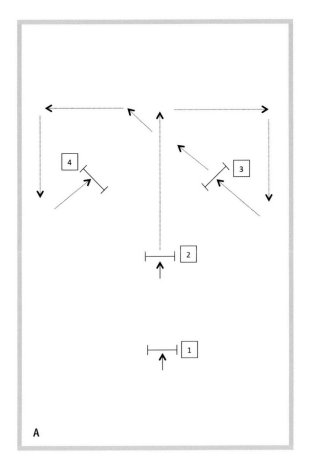

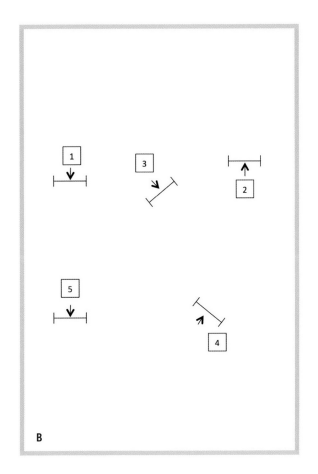

ROLLBACKS 2 A & B

NOTES: As in the previous exercises, set the fences in these exercises so they can be jumped in either direction and off either lead. The exercise in A is often used as part of an advanced equitation course. Exercise B is ridden mostly on the left lead, so at some point you need to reverse and go the opposite direction. Again, make sure you have adequate room between the fences and the rail in order to safely negotiate the turns.

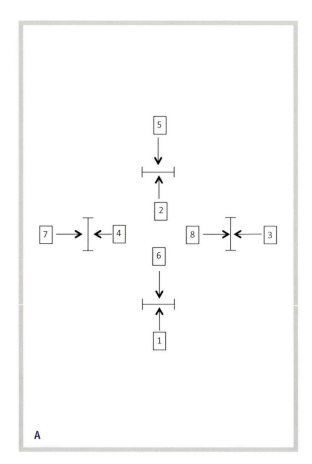

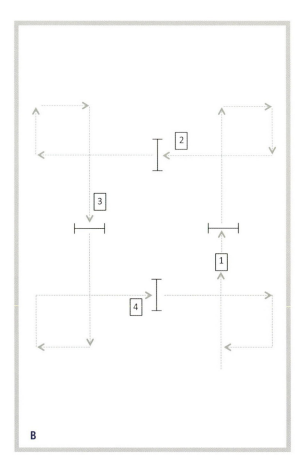

You need to set the fences for more advanced exercises so that you have adequate room to turn and get straight to the subsequent jump. Set them so they can be jumped in either direction, and use fewer filler elements to ensure they are easy to move around and adjust.

TECHNICAL EXERCISES A & B

NOTES: These exercises emphasize looking ahead and steering. Make sure that your ring is wide enough to allow for sweeping turns before you try to set them. The entire exercise in A is ridden from the left lead first. You must then reverse the pattern and practice off the right lead, as well. The exercise in B consists of "illegal" reverse turns. While you would never make turns like these in the show ring, they are a fun exercise and great for improving your ability to keep a consistent canter stride while turning.

A

B

SPACE-SAVING CONFIGURATIONS AND COURSES FOR SMALL ARENAS

The courses in this section are intended to provide those with smaller arenas or minimal jump components some ideas in how to set safe and useful schooling courses for jumping practice. They do assume that you have a basic jump inventory, including seven pairs of schooling standards and from 14 to 28 poles or other fill elements (see p. 53 for details). You should have an arena that is at least 150 feet long by 75 feet wide to allow you to set a four-stride line down the long side of the arena and make an adequate turn at either end.

Some of the courses described in the pages ahead are unconventional, at least in terms of what you typically see at horse shows, but they all follow the course design principals covered earlier in this book. As with larger courses, you should have at least one change of direction and at least one, single vertical fence. When you have a limited jump inventory, you will most likely have to use more vertical fences to allow you to create more jumps for your course. Another way to increase the number of jumping efforts in your course when you have a limited amount of equipment is to set the fences so they can be jumped from both directions. This means you will need ground lines on both sides of each fence. The courses in this

Setting courses in indoor arenas can present challenges in terms of space. I do not use wing standards in my indoor arena (pictured here), and I only use 10-foot poles. My trainer uses 8-foot poles in her indoor arena. Shorter poles not only conserve space, they have the added training benefit of forcing you to jump the center of each jump. You will find that after regularly schooling over 8-foot poles, the 12-foot poles used at horse shows appear very inviting.

This is close-up of a "multi-directional" standard. It allows you to place jump cups all the way around the post so one standard can make up one side for three separate jumps. Take note of the jump cups shown here: they are FEI-approved and will fall easily when hit. They can also be turned upside down when you need to use flat cups.

section assume that you have limited fill at your disposal; therefore, using ground lines, for both the horse and rider's depth perception, is important.

The distances between related obstacles are just as important over these courses designed for small space, if not more so, than when you set up in a larger space. Be aware that the horse's stride naturally shortens when the space is small, and pace and the quality of the canter is harder to maintain. The narrow width of the arena forces you to ride tighter turns (causing a natural loss of impulsion), and you have less time on the long sides or across the diagonal to get your horse straight to the jumps. Fences and lines set on the diagonal will most likely have sharper angles to them.

Taking all this into consideration, inside courses and those in small arenas often need to be set on a 10- to 11-foot average stride length in order for them to ride comfortably. Many of these "mini-courses" could really be considered gymnastic exercises, and as such you should set the fences using the recommended distances provided on p. 71 The courses in this section

do not include distances and are not drawn to scale; I leave it up to you to determine how to use the space you have available in order to meet the objectives that you have for your schooling while staying safe.

There is another consideration when setting courses in an indoor arena: the light level will probably be low. Use white or brightly colored poles and fill elements so the obstacles are easier to see, and avoid anything that blends in with the footing or the color of the walls. If the indoor you use for schooling has windows or skylights, take note of how shadows and sunspots may affect the visual aspect of the jumps.

Here are two angles of multi-directional wing standards and schooling standards in a three-jump, space-saving configuration. This kind of standard can be used to set any of the configurations provided in this section. The schooling standards save even more space and are less expensive than wings.

Space-Saving Configurations

Note: Square and rectangular outlines in these diagrams do not accurately represent the arena boundary. When setting the exercises in this section, make sure there is room for a safe approach to and landing from each fence, as well as space for turns between obstacles and the fence line or wall.

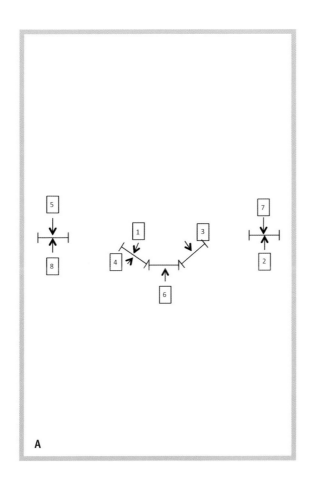

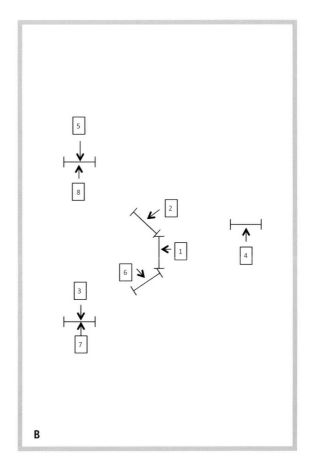

SPACE-SAVING CONFIGURATION 1 A & B: THE "U"

NOTES: These are configurations that I use frequently in my indoor arena. In order to use the configuration shown in B, your ring needs to be wide enough to handle the vertical fence set on the "centerline" (allow enough space for landing and a safe turn). When your ring is too narrow to accommodate the centerline jump, skip the jump set in the middle and make one of the other fences in the mini-course an oxer.

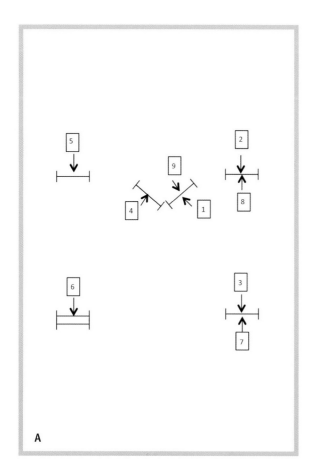

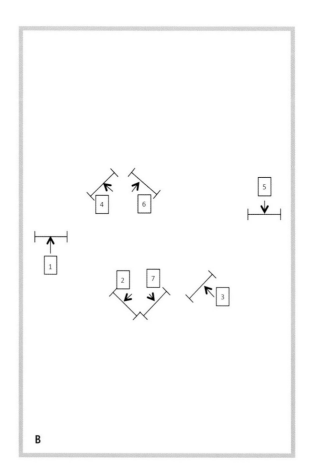

SPACE-SAVING CONFIGURATION 2 A & B: THE "V"

NOTES: Using a "V" configuration uses less space and gives you options for changing direction across the diagonal. Be careful to avoid interference with the outside tracks when you set this course. In exercise B, notice that fences #3 and #4 are set "square" because they are related obstacles. Fences #2, #6, and #7 are not related, so they need to be set so that they do not interfere with the other tracks.

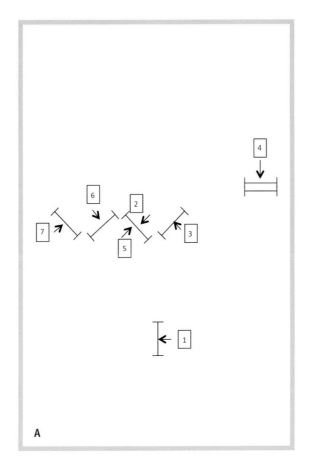

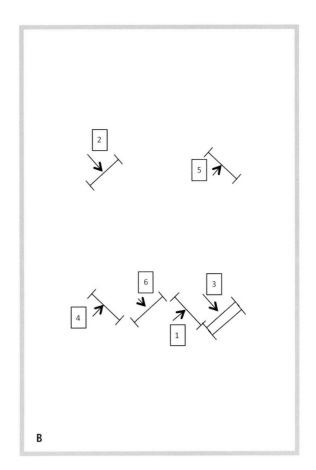

SPACE-SAVING CONFIGURATION 3 A & B: THE "W"

NOTES: These mini-courses feature four diagonally set fences. Depending upon the size of your arena, you can build a line off of some of these elements, as shown in B. This configuration is easier when set horizontally across the arena. When you set it vertically, it becomes quite difficult, especially when your arena is narrow (see p. 90).

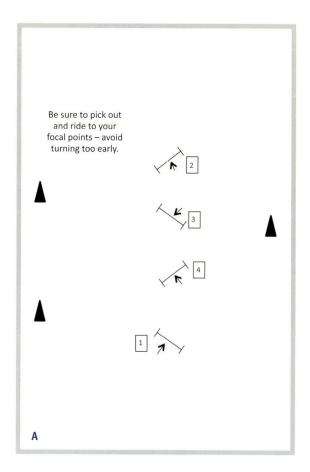

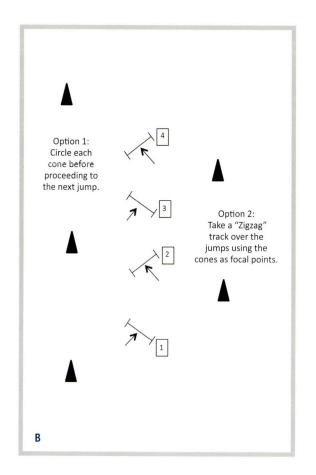

SPACE-SAVING CONFIGURATION 4 A & B: THE ADVANCED "W"

NOTES: In the two courses shown here, the "W" configuration is set vertically. Compare these to the mini-courses on p. 94. These gymnastic exercises are very difficult, especially when your ring is narrow. I recommend using only ground poles the first time. As a schooling exercise they can be used for improved steering and riding to a focal point. Technically, they incorporate broken lines and "illegal" reverse turns.

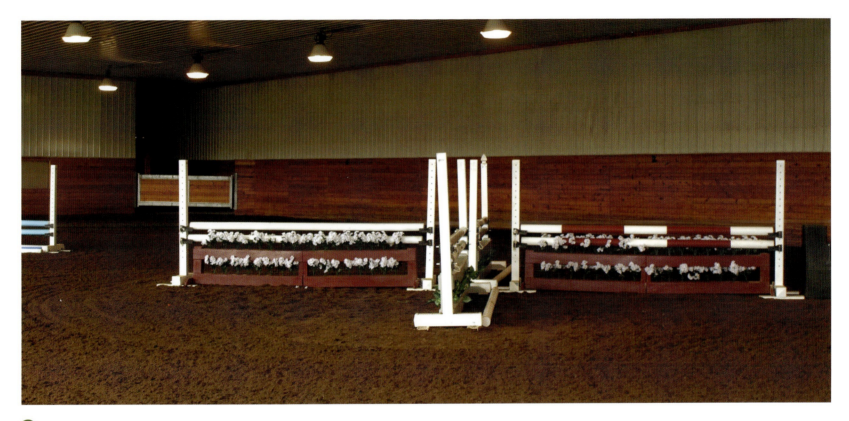

∧ I like to use this pinwheel configuration in my indoor arena. The striped poles are from Hi-Tech Horse Jumps, Inc, the US distributor for JUMP4JOY (www.hitechhorsejumps.com), and the brush boxes are from Burlingham Sports (www.burlinghamsports.com).

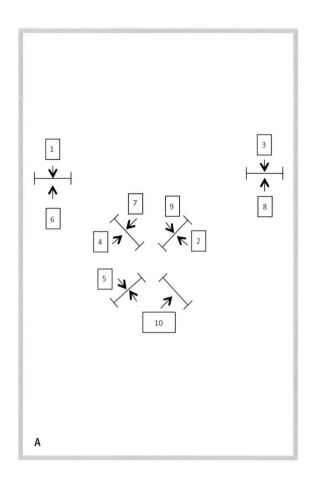

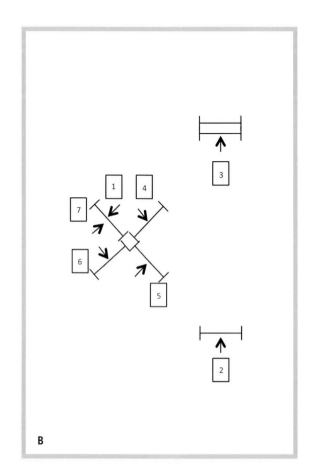

SPACE-SAVING CONFIGURATION 5 A & B: THE PINWHEEL

NOTES: Pinwheels are jumps set in an "X" configuration. The closer you set them, the tighter your turns will be. Some of the turns shown in these two mini-courses are reverse turns or rollbacks. These tracks are for more advanced horses and riders.

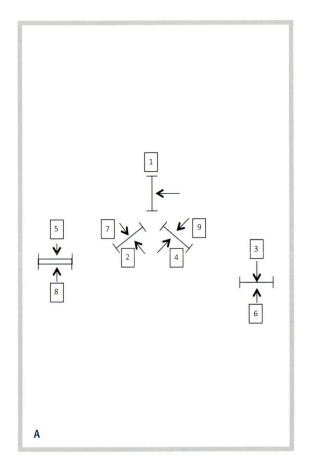

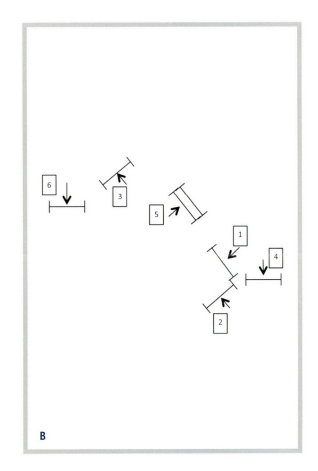

SPACE-SAVING CONFIGURATION 6 A & B: THE "Y"

NOTES: The "Y" gives you two single fences, one off either lead so you can practice changing to/from both directions. When your ring is narrow, you may not be able to set Fence #1 on the centerline as shown in the configuration in A.

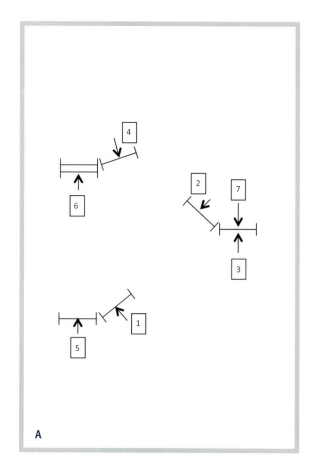

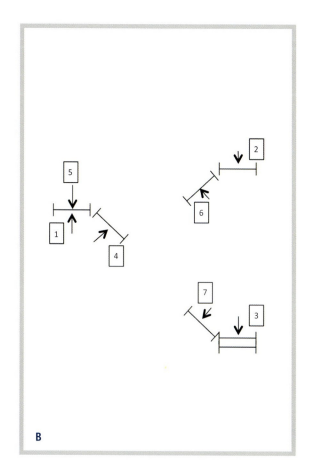

SPACE-SAVING CONFIGURATION 7 A & B: THE "DOG LEG"

NOTES: A "dog leg" is a configuration where jump standards are set next to each other in order to minimize "dead space" between jumps that is not otherwise needed for your track.

> This indoor mini-course features jumps set with alternating angles.

SPACE-SAVING CONFIGURATION 8 A & B: ALTERNATING ANGLES

NOTES: The alternating angles configuration is very similar to the "W" (see p. 95), but it only uses three diagonally set fences rather than four.

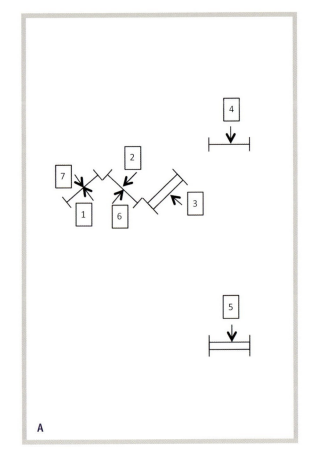

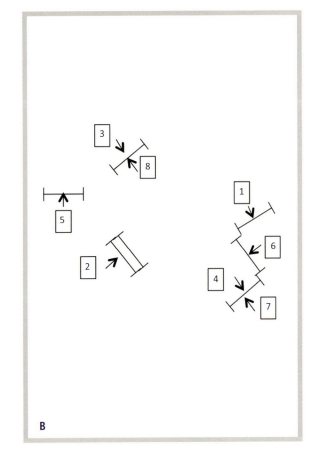

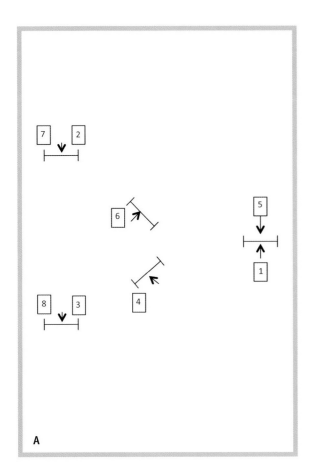

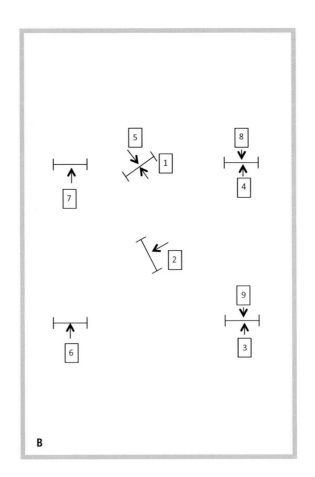

Note: Square and rectangular outlines in these diagrams do not accurately represent the arena boundary. When setting the exercises in this section, make sure there is room for a safe approach to and landing from each fence, as well as space for turns between obstacles and the fence line or wall.

SMALL ARENA COURSE 1 A & B

NOTES: These two mini-courses both follow a simple side/diagonal/side track and only use vertical fences (no spreads). The lines should be set far enough off the rail so you have room for the track you need to take to and from the single diagonal fences.

Use the diagrams for mini-courses as a guide; actual placement of the jumps in your course will be determined by the length of your poles and whether or not you use schooling or wing standards. The panel jumps shown here are from Premier Equestrian (www.premierequestrian.net). The grey PVC culvert gates and "mini" Liverpool are from JUMPVC (www.jumpvc.com).

SMALL ARENA COURSE 2 A & B

NOTES: Both these mini-courses feature two oxers: one as part of a line, and one set as a single fence.

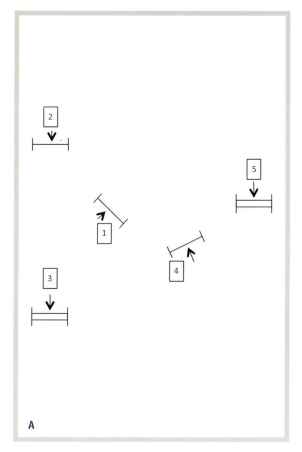

A

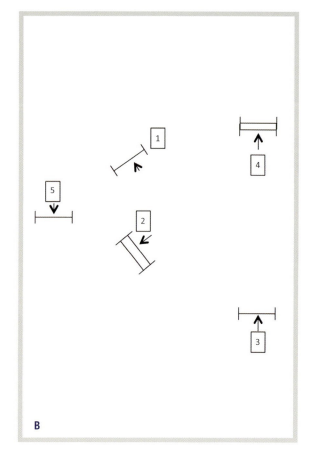

B

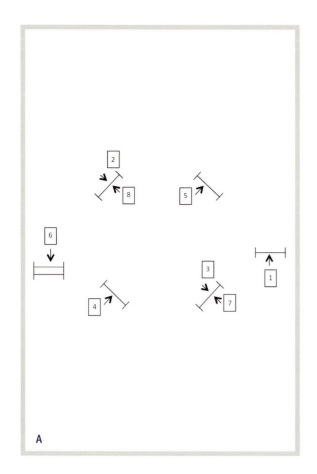

A

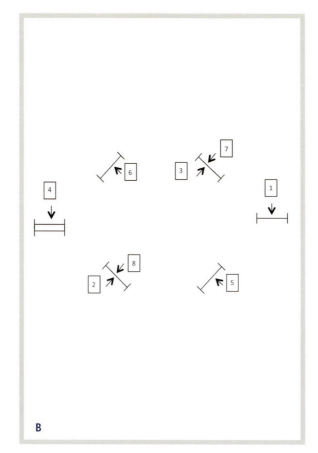

B

Here is a simple five-stride line, vertical to oxer, set up indoors. (The photo is deceiving— there was plenty of room to land and turn after the oxer.) Yellow is a good color to use indoors as it contrasts well with the lower light level found naturally inside.

SMALL ARENA COURSE 3 A & B

NOTES: Here are two basic side/diagonal/side mini-courses with diagonal lines used to change direction and a single oxer. These show how the same diagram and setup can be used to create different courses.

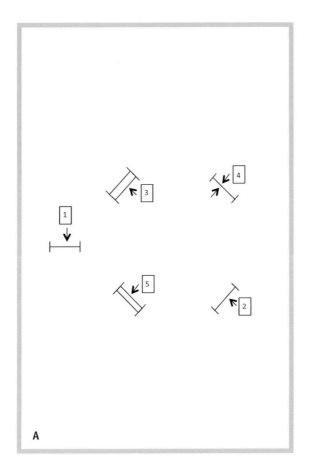

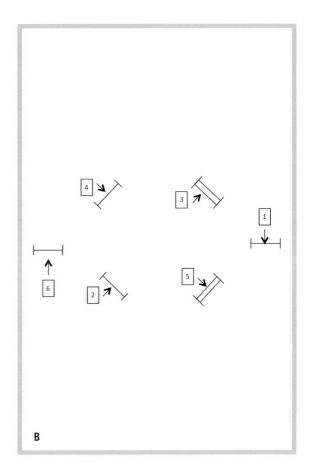

SMALL ARENA COURSE 4 A & B

NOTES: Two basic side/diagonal/side mini-courses with diagonal lines used to change direction and two oxers.

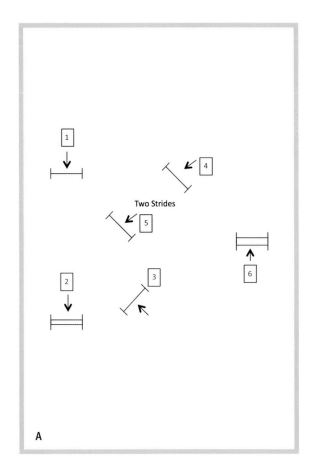

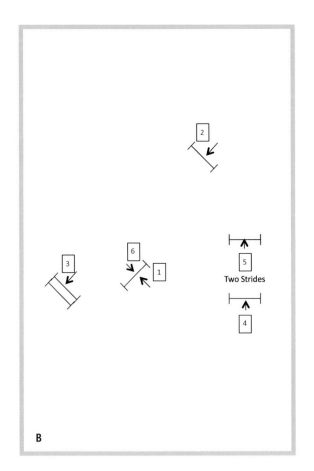

SMALL ARENA COURSE 5 A & B

NOTES: These mini-courses introduce a vertical to vertical combination, one on the diagonal (A) and one on a straight line (B).

Here you can see a good setup for an indoor Liverpool (water tray). The bottom of the Liverpool is shiny, making it appear as if it has water in it, and two white poles, one placed on either side of the Liverpool, provide ground lines to give this fence some dimension. (The Liverpool and striped poles are from Hi-Tech Horse Jumps— www.hitechhorsejumps.com.)

SMALL ARENA COURSE 6 A & B

NOTES: : These mini-courses introduce a combination, both set diagonally across the ring. One is off the left lead (A), and the other off the right (B). One course uses a vertical to oxer combination (A) and the other hasa vertical to vertical combination (B).

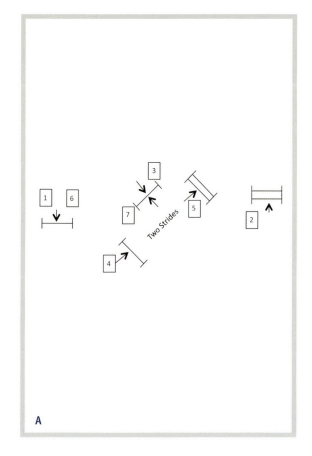

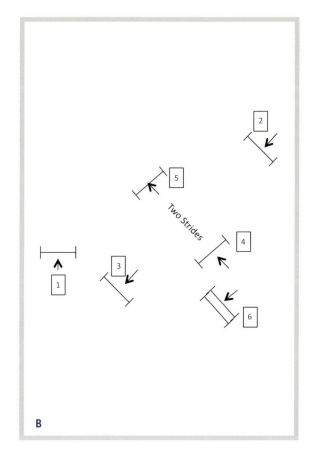

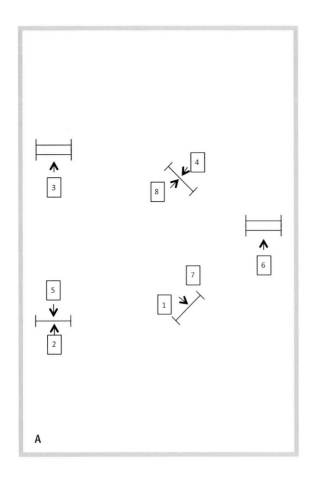

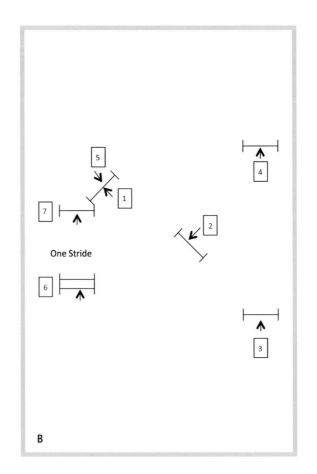

SMALL ARENA COURSE 7 A & B

NOTES: These two mini-courses introduce a few more challenges! In A there is a broken line between Fence #4 and #5 (you have to change leads between obstacles). This is followed by a moderate rollback turn between Fence #6 and #7 (around #4 and #8). When traveling from Fence #7 to #8 take the track along the rail so you travel between #2 and #5. In B there is a one-stride combination with an oxer as the first element—tricky! You can change the dynamics of the course by altering the order of the elements and adding more strides to the length of the combination.

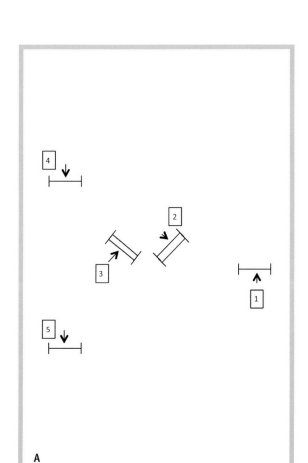

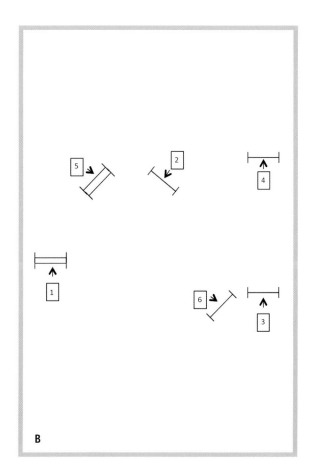

SMALL ARENA COURSE 8 A & B

NOTES: The mini-course in A has two single oxers set on the diagonal, while the course in B also features two oxers—one as Fence #1, and one as the first fence in the final line. In A, travel between Fence #5 and the rail when proceeding from Fence #2 to #3.

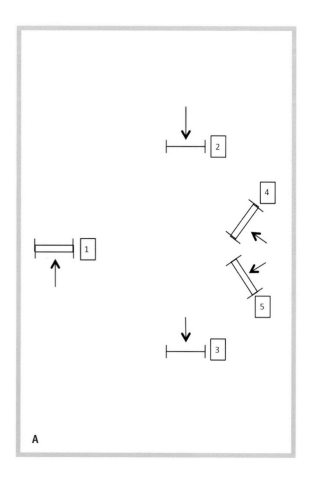

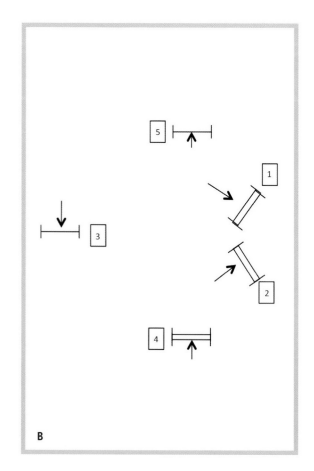

SMALL ARENA COURSE 9 A & B

NOTES: These two mini-courses include three single oxer fences. When designing a course that includes oxers, you generally don't want more than "two of a kind" in succession. So, after two verticals, the next fence should be an oxer, and vice versa. (The exception might be a combination, but the fence before, and then after, the combination should be of a different type.) The angled fences shown here may be close to the side of your arena, depending upon its width. Make sure you set the fences so you have adequate room for takeoff and landing, and that you do not have to jump a fence at an angle.

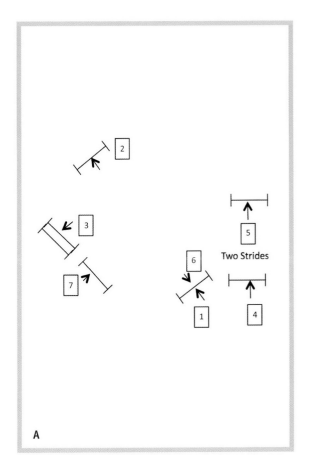

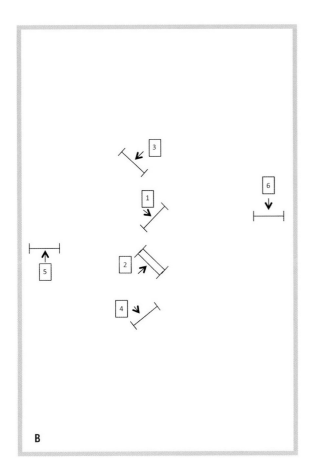

SMALL ARENA COURSE 10 A & B

NOTES: In A, the mini-course starts on a diagonal line with a rollback to Fence #3, which is followed by a combination with another rollback to Fence #6. The course in B gets more technical with a vertically set "W" configuration (see p. 94). Your horse should be capable of automatic flying lead changes before you attempt these courses, both of which are modeled after what would be seen in the jumper or equitation ring.

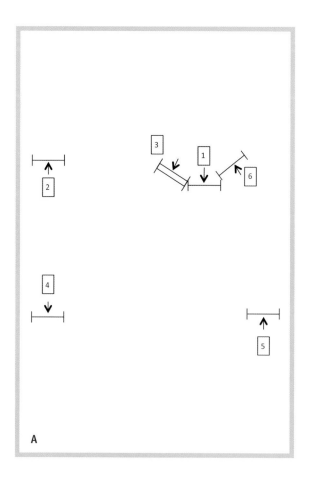

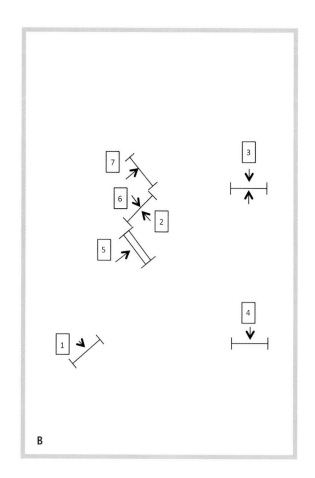

SMALL ARENA COURSE 11 A & B

NOTES: The mini-course in A has a rollback from Fence #1 to #2 and a broken line from Fence #3 to #4, followed by a bending line from Fence #5 to #6. In B you have several rollback turns, again making these more jumper- or equitation-style courses and fairly difficult.

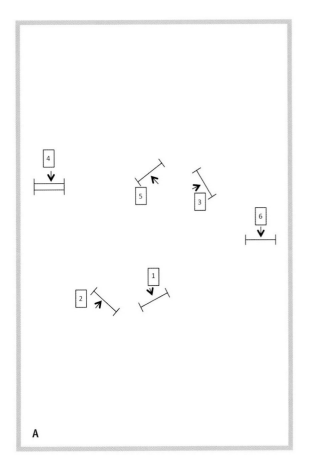

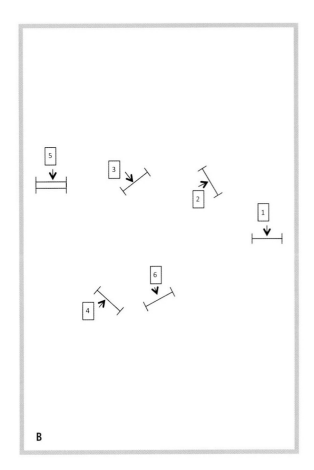

SMALL ARENA COURSE 12 A & B

NOTES: These two setups are the same, they just follow different tracks. If you do not have adequate room for the turns suggested here, eliminate one or two of the jumps.

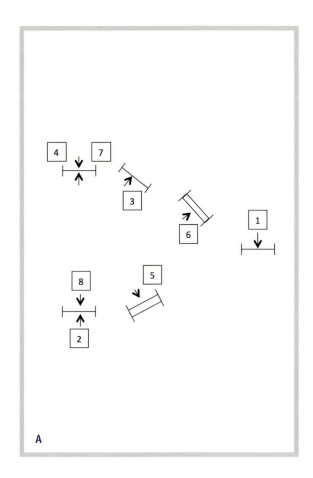

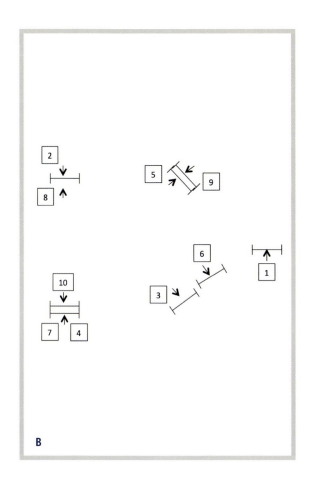

SMALL ARENA COURSE 13 A & B

NOTES: These two mini-courses are set to emphasize bending lines. Leave enough room to make the turns and to ride between the outside line and the rail.

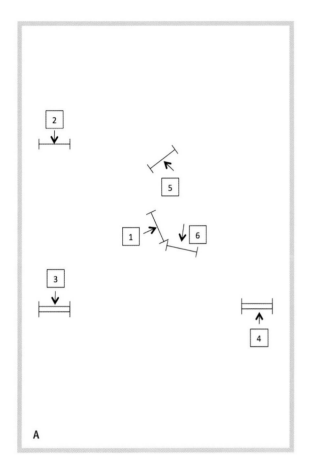

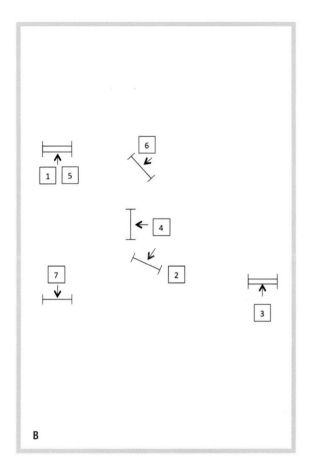

SMALL ARENA COURSE 14 A & B

NOTES: These two mini-courses are good for schooling jumpers or equitation riders. The course in A is a little less complex, while B features an "S" turn (two alternating 90-degree turns), which is sometimes included in advanced equitation courses. As with other courses in a small space, allow enough room for approaches, takeoffs, landings, and turns.

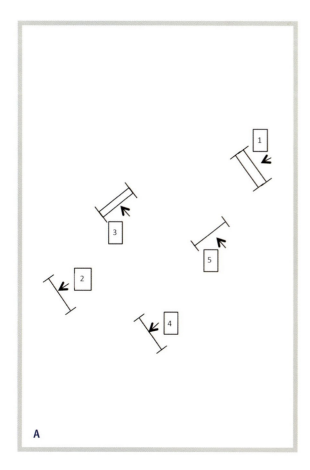

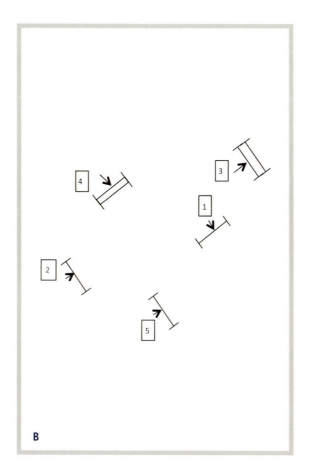

SMALL ARENA COURSE 15 A & B

NOTES: These examples offer fairly simple setups with one diagonal line that you can jump oxer to vertical (A) or vertical to oxer (B). Be prepared to set a "mirror image" of either of these courses during your week's schooling, so that you get equal practice off both leads.

> Even when setting mini-courses indoors, you can still add some creative and decorative touches to make your schooling scenarios more like show situations, and to ensure that a schooling course that may be up for several days running is attractive and pleasing to others in your boarding or training facility. Here are examples of simple holiday decorations for a festive touch.

A

B

7

Specialty Courses
Hunters, Equitation, Advanced Gymnastics, and Jumpers

- **Hunter Courses**
- **Equitation Courses**
- **Advanced Gymnastics**
- **Jumper Courses**

The full courses contained in rest of this book are divided into discipline-specific groupings: hunter, equitation, advanced gymnastics, and jumpers. These courses assume that you have a "full course" of jump material, including about 10 to 15 sets of standards and the appropriate number of poles and filler, such as gates, hurdles, and boxes. However, don't be discouraged if you don't have a large enough material inventory to set them exactly as they appear. It is of training benefit to set all the courses using just ground poles in order to practice pace and track,

Jump courses for different disciplines have different looks: hunter course (A); equitation course (B); jumper course (C).

or you can divide the courses up, setting four or more of the jumps in the sequence presented, and then moving those jumps around to practice a different skill. Keep in mind that, as I mentioned earlier in this book, most jumping programs are not about jumping an entire course over and over, but about working on a few specific skills at a time over a small number of jumps.

Each of the remaining sections begins with a description of what to expect in a specific division at a horse show, and I also explain tests that are commonly asked. In some places, I have included information from the 2011–2012 USEF/USHJA Rulebook regarding course design requirements for the divisions (and some specific classes), but please know that those of you who show should regularly consult the current edition of the Rulebook, as well as the prize list for specific competitions, as rules change from show to show and from time to time. I do not provide instruction on how to ride the courses ahead. As stated throughout this book, seek a professional trainer when you need help.

As with the grids, gymnastics, and mini-courses (see pp. 69-116), each course provided has a few notes on the

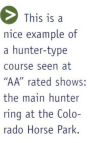

> This is a nice example of a hunter-type course seen at "AA" rated shows: the main hunter ring at the Colorado Horse Park.

skill(s) it emphasizes and what to watch for when setting it. The courses are drawn for an arena approximately 100 by 200 feet and assume that the width of the jumps is 10 feet. Distances and other measurements are not specified because each arena, horse, and rider will vary, so you will need to determine what is appropriate for where you school and who else will be using the course. (Revisit the chapter on distances for a refresher—see p. 21.) Do note that if your arena has dramatically different dimensions than those assumed here, or if you use big wing standards or 12-foot poles, you *will* have to alter the layout of these courses. The diagrams I provide may serve as inspiration to you, while the knowledge you've gathered so far in this book will allow you to make them your own, as well as safe and appropriate for your own schooling program and that of your friends and barnmates.

HUNTER COURSES

Hunter courses are designed to simulate obstacles and conditions that would be found when foxhunting over open terrain. The objective of a hunter course is to showcase the horse's ground-covering gallop, calm demeanor, brilliant way of going, and classic jumping style. Hunter classes at a horse show are judged subjectively on this criteria.

∧ A nicely appointed vertical fence in the hunter ring.

∧ This is a beautifully decorated hunter-type fence, using fresh sod, real ferns, and cut logs as standards. The poles and gates are painted to look like birch/aspen limbs. This jump was used in the International Hunter Derby Class at the Colorado Horse Park in 2011.

Division	Eligibility	Fence Height
Baby Green Hunters	Open to horses who have not shown 3' or higher.	2'6" to 2'9"
Pre-Green Working Hunters	Open to horses who will be eligible to show in the First Year Green Division in subsequent years. A horse may only show as a Pre-Green horse for two years.	3' Section and 3'3" Section
Conformation Hunters	Judged 70% Performance, 30% Conformation.	3'6" Green Section and 3'9" Regular Section
Green Working Hunter	A horse can show one year in each section.	3'6" First Year Green Section and 3'9" Second Year Green Section
Performance Working Hunter	Open to all horses and riders.	3'3" Section and 3'6" - 3'9" Section
High Performance Working Hunter	Open to all horses and riders (replaced the Regular Working Hunter Division).	4'0" - 4'6"
Hunter Classics (sometimes referred to as National Hunter Derbies)	Offered as an additional "money" class. Usually eligibility and fence heights are the same as the related division (i.e. Pre-Green, Green or Performance or High Performance Working Hunter). Classics may be held for Children's, Amateur and Amateur Owner as well as the Pony Divisions.	Same as the height for the related division.
International Hunter Derbies	Open to all horses and riders. The Derbies are the "Grand Prix" for the Hunters. Each Derby consists of two rounds: the Hunter Classic Round and the Handy Hunter Round. The minimum purse for an International Hunter Derby is $10,000.	Fence Height is 3'6" - 3'9" with at least four 4'0" option fences. Fences can be as high as 4'6".

▲ Commonly offered fence heights and classes in the hunter divisions. Note: Review the USEF/USHJA Rulebook, show prize list, and/or regional rules before entering any division at a horse show.

Division	Eligibility	Fence Height
Children's Hunters	Open to horses and ponies ridden by a junior exhibitor. Each horse show may have cross entry restrictions for showing in both the Children's and Junior Divisions.	3'0"
Junior Hunter Division	Open to Junior Riders.	3'6"
Children's Hunter Pony	Open to ponies ridden by a junior exhibitor. Show may have cross entry restrictions for showing in the regular pony divisions.	Small/Medium (under 13.2 hands) 2'0" Large (over 13.2 hands) 2'6"
Pony Working Hunters	Open to Junior Riders.	Small (under 12.2 hands) 2'3" Medium (over 12.2 hands not exceeding 13.2 hands) 2'6" Large (over 13.2 hands not exceeding 14.2 hands) 3'0"
Adult Amateur Hunter	Open to amateur riders 18 year of age or older who are no longer eligible to compete as a junior. Each show may have restrictions regarding the cross entry of a rider or horse/rider combination from showing in both the Adult Amateur and Amateur Owner divisions.	3'0"
Amateur Owner Working Hunters	Open to amateur riders 18 years of age or older who are no longer eligible to compete as a junior. Ownership of the horse must be by the rider or the rider's family.	3'3" Low A/O Section 3'6" Regular A/O Section

▲ Commonly offered fence heights and classes for children, juniors, and amateurs in the hunter divisions. Note: Review the USEF/USHJA Rulebook, show prize list, and/or regional rules before entering any division at a horse show.

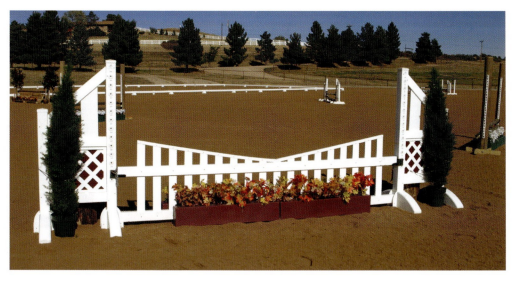

This type of gate, with pickets on top rather than a smooth finish, should always have a pole placed over it. The picket gate is from Burlingham Sports (www.burlinghamsports.com) and the standards are from Premier Equestrian (www.premierequestrian.net).

Courses in hunter divisions feature natural-looking gates, coops, roll tops, walls, boxes, hedges, and lots of foliage. Vertical fences are built in a specific manner: a gate with one rail over it, plus a set of small boxes (or a short wall) in front of the gate, with a very short pair of flower boxes as a ground line. Oxers have an additional set of standards added behind the gate and a single pole set in an ascending height (ramped). You do not see square (front and back poles are equal height) or Swedish (top poles slanted in opposite directions) oxers on a hunter course.

Lower-level hunter courses often follow a figure-eight pattern, sometimes referred to as a *side/diagonal/side* track, such as the ones I described in chapter 6 (see p. 103). The first fence in a hunter line is typically a vertical fence, with an ascending oxer as the second obstacle. There is generally at least one single oxer included in the course.

As the fence heights go up in the hunter ring, you will often see one- or two-stride combinations either by themselves or as part of a longer line. Bending lines are also common in the higher divisions of hunter classes.

HANDY HUNTER

Handy hunter courses may also include bending and broken lines, as well as rollbacks. A handy hunter course is usually galloped, or ridden with more pace, and includes elements that give the rider an opportunity to

This fence, in this case part of a handy hunter course, is called a "Riviera gate" (made by JumPVC— www.jumpvc.com). When turned over so the arch is at the bottom rather than the top (and this particular gate is made to be hung either way), it is called a "viaduct" or "Culvert gate."

demonstrate rideability or "handiness." A trot fence is also a common element, and sometimes the requirement to open and close a gate is included. The horse should promptly and easily lengthen or shorten his stride and change gaits. He should be able to make tight, balanced turns. Handy hunter courses often follow a track and contain tests that are similar to what you would see in the equitation ring but are judged on the ability of the horse to jump freely, without the interference of the rider.

Here is a two-stride combination in a hunter derby class and a nice example of a bank jump in the upper left-hand corner.

HUNTER DERBY

Hunter derbies, which were first held at major horse shows in 2009, are meant to be technical in nature and not only require rollbacks, trot fences, and long gallops to unrelated distances, they frequently have *option fences* set at different heights, as well as optional tracks. Fences can be airy or imposing, and include "natural" fence types that you might see on the hunt field: Aikens (brush and logs), large hedges, roll tops, coops, brush boxes, banks, water, and "creative fences" that simulate farm or open country settings. Courses are designed so that the approaches to jumps vary greatly, from short, to long, to serpentine. Often the decision on the specific track and/or fence to ride is left up to the rider, and the rider is rewarded for choosing a more difficult route and planning the best strategy to produce a brilliant performance in her and her horse. Balance, straightness, and good jumping style are still important, but horses who are daring, athletic, and show some expression will be rewarded.

The *National Hunter Derby* is an introduction to the derby for-

Obstacles in hunter derby courses must simulate those reminiscent of the hunt field. The course must offer a variety of "classic" jumps with different appearances, including post-and-rail obstacles, coops, stone walls, hedges, logs, ditches, and banks. This bank can be jumped from all four directions. A bank usually requires you to either jump up or jump down it—technically, this example is called a "table" because the horse will jump up the bank, take a couple of strides on the flat part of the "table top," and then jump down (or up) the other side.

> Photographs of the hunter derby course provided on p. 138. Note in B that both hunter- and jumper-type fences are shown; for schooling, it can be of benefit to mix up element type so riders can school over a variety of obstacles.

mat for hunters, and bridges the gap between the classic hunter courses and the highest level of derby competition, the *International Hunter Derby*. While the format for the National and International Derbies is similar, fence heights and prize money are lower on the national level. Each International Hunter Derby consists of two rounds: the *Hunter Classic Round* (judged on style and brilliance) and the *Handy Hunter Round* (judged on style, brilliance, and rideability).

The International Hunter Derby was created with the hope that the derbies would return the hunters to their hunt-field roots, take the hunters to an international level, and promote hunters as a spectator sport, thus being worthy of sponsorship opportunities. Derbies are to hunters what Grand Prix classes are to jumpers.

◀ "Brego" owned by Lisa Martinez-Bates jumps this "snake fence" nicely. This type of option fence that can be jumped from both directions is often used in hunter derby classes. When used for schooling, it conserves space, uses fewer jump components, and offers the benefit of practicing multiple track options.

▼ High/low option fences from an International Hunter Derby class.

Hunter Courses

BEGINNER HUNTER COURSE 1

NOTES: This is about as simple as a course can get. All fences are single verticals, no lines, and no oxers. It starts with a straight approach to Fence #1. Following that, there is a long approach to each of the remaining obstacles. Ground lines should be set on both sides of each fence so they can be jumped from either direction.

COURSE COMPOSITION	
5	Total Number of Obstacles
5	Total Number of Verticals
0	Total Number of Oxers
5	Wing Standards (pairs)
0	Schooling Standards (pairs)
5	Filler Items
10	Poles (less if fillers are used)
8	Ground Lines or Flower Boxes
20	Jump Cups

Note: The courses in this chapter are created with a horizontal orientation (see p. 39). Square and rectangular outlines in these diagrams do not accurately represent the arena boundary. When setting the exercises in this section, make sure there is room for a safe approach to and landing from each fence, as well as space for turns between obstacles and the fence line or wall.

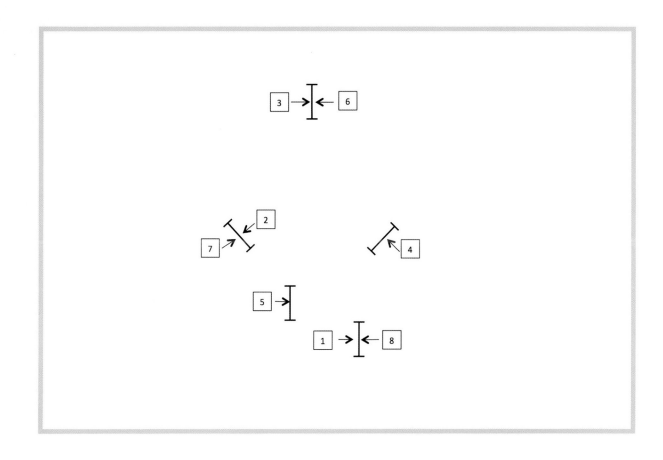

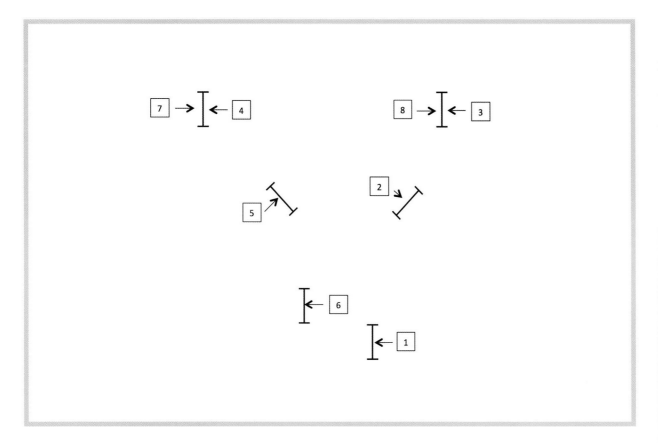

BEGINNER HUNTER COURSE 2

NOTES: Set all fences so they can be jumped from both directions, using ground lines on both sides. Use only vertical fences, no oxers. Set this introduction to a line so that it is parallel to the arena rail/wall. This will help you keep your horse straight between the related elements. It is slightly easier to introduce a line on a straight side than across the diagonal.

COURSE COMPOSITION	
6	Total Number of Obstacles
6	Total Number of Verticals
0	Total Number of Oxers
6	Wing Standards (pairs)
0	Schooling Standards (pairs)
6	Filler Items
12	Poles (less if fillers are used)
8	Ground Lines or Flower Boxes
24	Jump Cups

BEGINNER HUNTER COURSE 3

NOTES: Set all fences so that they can be jumped from both directions with the exception of the single ascending oxer, using ground lines on both sides of each vertical. This course starts on a diagonal vertical fence and ends with the introduction of an ascending oxer that can only be jumped off the left lead going toward the upper right-hand corner of the course diagram.

COURSE COMPOSITION	
7	Total Number of Obstacles
6	Total Number of Verticals
1	Total Number of Oxers
7	Wing Standards (pairs)
1	Schooling Standards (pairs)
7	Filler Items
15	Poles (less if fillers are used)
7	Ground Lines or Flower Boxes
30	Jump Cups

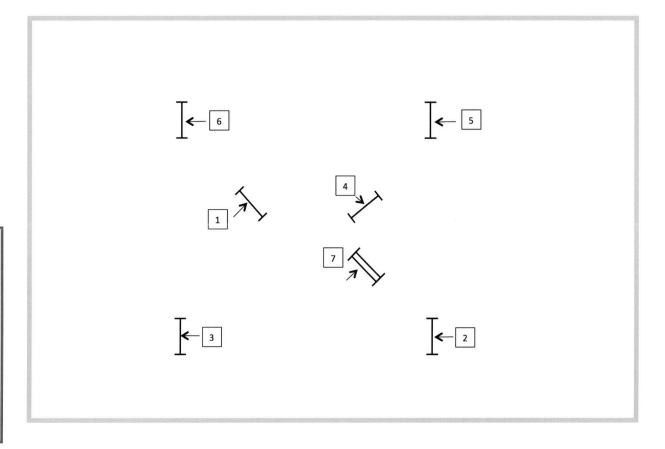

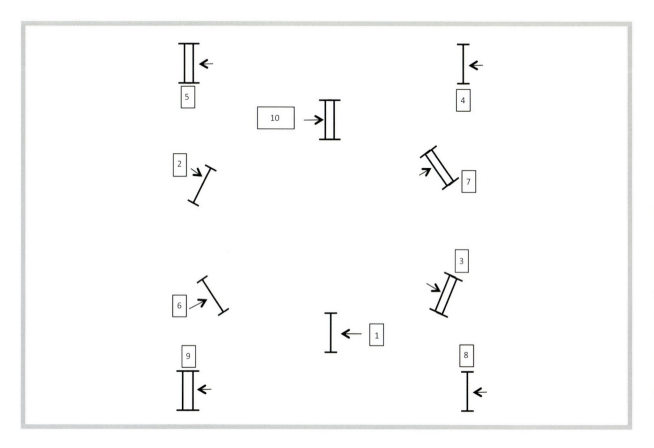

BASIC HUNTER COURSE 1

NOTES: Here is a simple side/diagonal/side course. It uses more jumps than you need for a beginner course, so if you have limited space in your arena, shorten the length of the diagonal lines or remove one of the single fences to give you more room to move the outside lines in toward the center of the ring.

COURSE COMPOSITION	
10	Total Number of Obstacles
5	Total Number of Verticals
5	Total Number of Oxers
10	Wing Standards (pairs)
5	Schooling Standards (pairs)
10	Filler Items
25	Poles (less if fillers are used)
10	Ground Lines or Flower Boxes
50	Jump Cups

BASIC HUNTER COURSE 2

NOTES: Even though all of the lines in this course are symmetrical and should ride in the same number of strides, the physical distance of the lines may need to be adjusted by a few feet to accommodate inclines or declines and depending whether the line tracks toward or away from the in-gate.

COURSE COMPOSITION	
9	Total Number of Obstacles
5	Total Number of Verticals
4	Total Number of Oxers
9	Wing Standards (pairs)
4	Schooling Standards (pairs)
9	Filler Items
22	Poles (less if fillers are used)
9	Ground Lines or Flower Boxes
44	Jump Cups

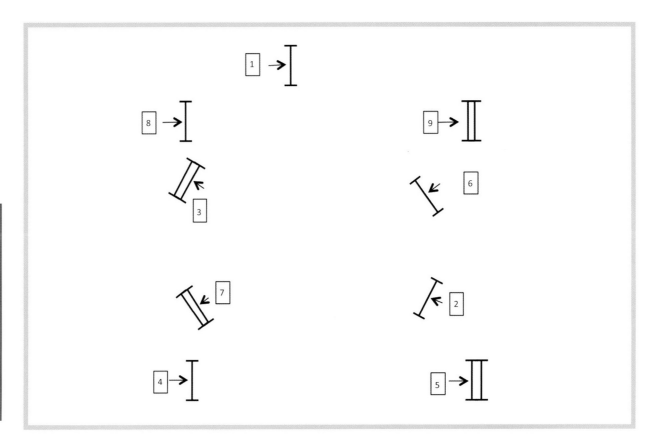

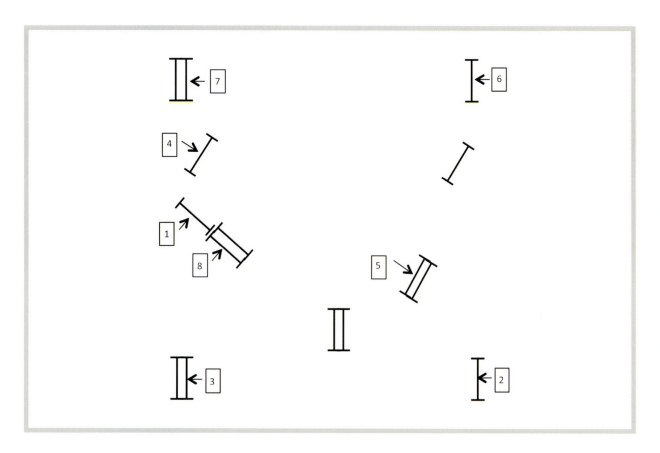

BASIC HUNTER COURSE 3

NOTES: This course actually has more fences than you need for any one course (an additional single vertical and an additional single oxer), but setting them provides "options" for schooling purposes.

COURSE COMPOSITION	
10	Total Number of Obstacles
5	Total Number of Verticals
5	Total Number of Oxers
10	Wing Standards (pairs)
5	Schooling Standards (pairs)
10	Filler Items
25	Poles (less if fillers are used)
10	Ground Lines or Flower Boxes
50	Jump Cups

INTERMEDIATE HUNTER COURSE 1

NOTES: This course differs from a traditional hunter setup in that both diagonal
lines are jumped off the right lead and
both outside lines are jumped off the left
lead. Usually, a hunter course is set so
that one diagonal line is jumped off the
left lead and the other off the right, and
one outside line is jumped off the left and
the other off the right. Here you also have
a combination made up of two vertical
fences set two strides apart—the most
common combination seen in the hunter
ring. Notice that, as mentioned earlier in
the book, for hunter courses, fences in a
combination are numbered consecutively
rather than using the letter designation
("a," "b," "c") seen in jumper and
equitation rings.

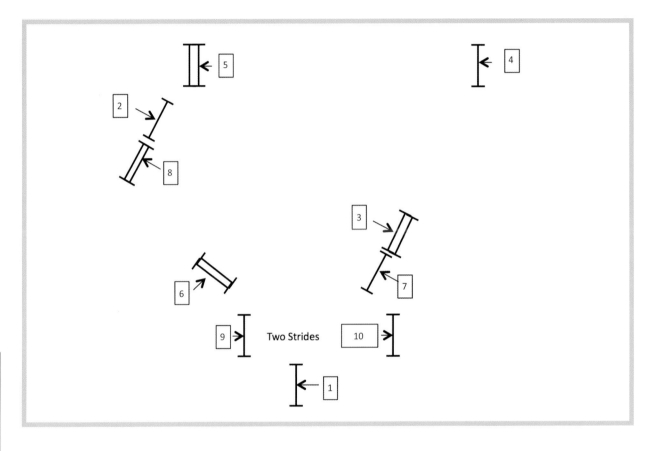

COURSE COMPOSITION	
10	Total Number of Obstacles
6	Total Number of Verticals
4	Total Number of Oxers
10	Wing Standards (pairs)
4	Schooling Standards (pairs)
10	Filler Items
24	Poles (less if fillers are used)
10	Ground Lines or Flower Boxes
48	Jump Cups

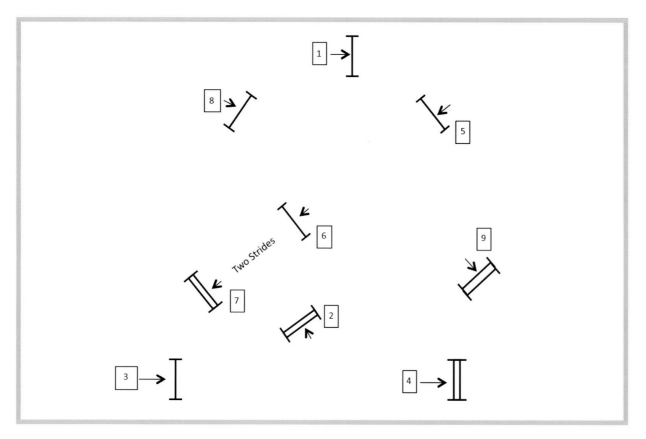

INTERMEDIATE HUNTER COURSE 2

NOTES: This course has incorporated a bending line (Fence #8 to #9) that should be at least five, but preferably six strides or longer if you have the room. Remember when setting the distances for these more advanced lines that curving lines cause the horse's stride to shorten slightly.

COURSE COMPOSITION	
9	Total Number of Obstacles
5	Total Number of Verticals
4	Total Number of Oxers
9	Wing Standards (pairs)
4	Schooling Standards (pairs)
9	Filler Items
22	Poles (less if fillers are used)
9	Ground Lines or Flower Boxes
44	Jump Cups

INTERMEDIATE HUNTER COURSE 3

NOTES: You will seldom see a one-stride combination (Fence #4 to #5) in the hunter ring, but they are legal. Set one up on your practice courses from time to time so it isn't a big surprise when one appears at a horse show!

COURSE COMPOSITION	
8	Total Number of Obstacles
5	Total Number of Verticals
3	Total Number of Oxers
8	Wing Standards (pairs)
3	Schooling Standards (pairs)
8	Filler Items
19	Poles (less if fillers are used)
8	Ground Lines or Flower Boxes
38	Jump Cups

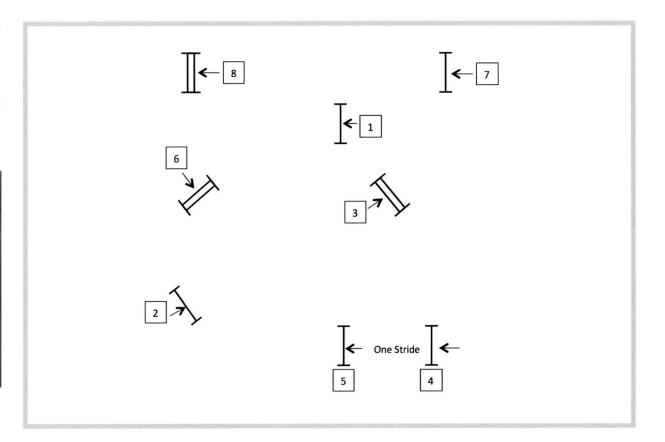

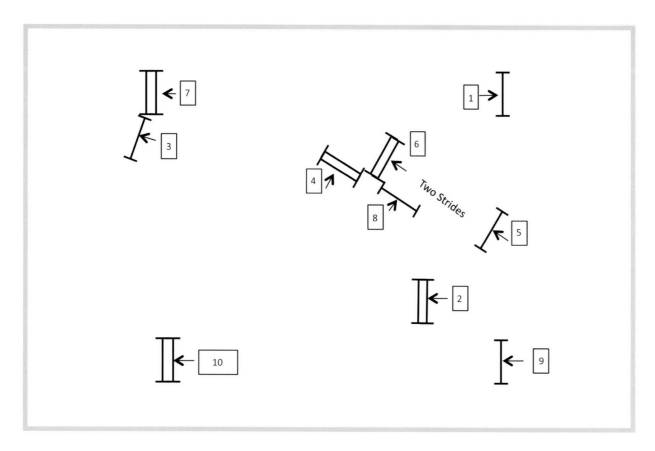

HANDY HUNTER COURSE 1

NOTES: Assume that the in-gate is in the lower left hand corner of this course diagram. In a handy hunter round, you want to be able to gallop directly to the first fence without making a courtesy circle. In this course, Fence #1 is positioned so that it is possible to take a direct track to it. Set Fence #1 so it can be jumped either direction—then you can use it later as part of a straight line, should you choose.

COURSE COMPOSITION	
10	Total Number of Obstacles
5	Total Number of Verticals
5	Total Number of Oxers
10	Wing Standards (pairs)
5	Schooling Standards (pairs)
10	Filler Items
25	Poles (less if fillers are used)
10	Ground Lines or Flower Boxes
50	Jump Cups

HANDY HUNTER COURSE 2

NOTES: A handy hunter course must have two changes of directions and at least one combination and three of the following: a hand gallop to a jump (usually a single oxer); a bending line; a rollback turn (in this course, a left-lead rollback from Fence #1 to Fence #2 and right-lead rollback from Fence #3 to Fence #4); a fence at the end of the ring (Fence #4); a gate to open from the saddle; or a trot over one obstacle not to exceed two-and-a-half feet (Fence #9).

COURSE COMPOSITION

9	Total Number of Obstacles
6	Total Number of Verticals
3	Total Number of Oxers
9	Wing Standards (pairs)
3	Schooling Standards (pairs)
9	Filler Items
21	Poles (less if fillers are used)
9	Ground Lines or Flower Boxes
42	Jump Cups

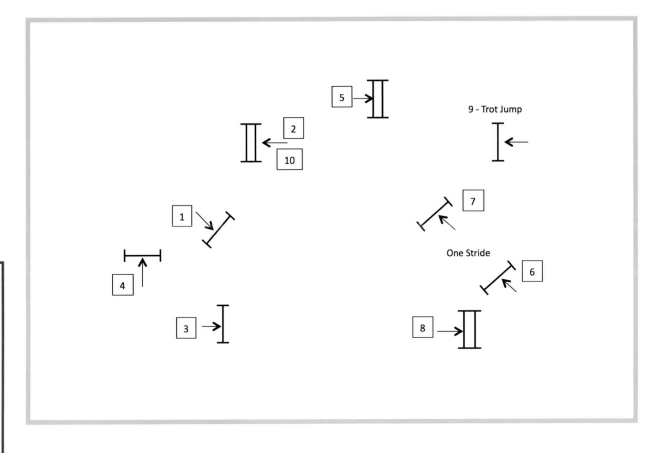

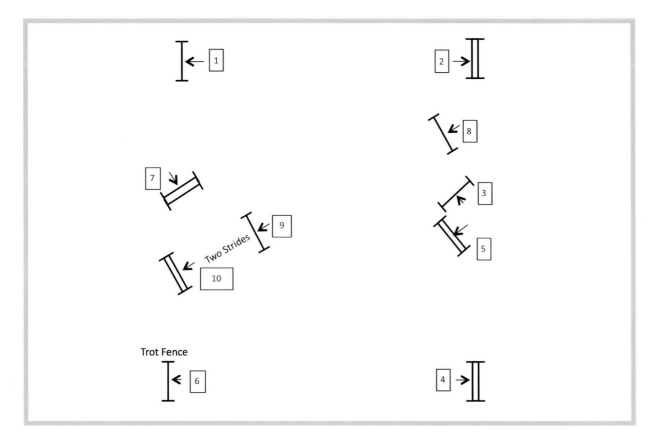

HANDY HUNTER COURSE 3

NOTES: This course has rollback turns from Fence #2 to #3, #3 to #4, and #4 to #5. The final line is five strides to a combination. In hunter classes, when you have a line to a combination, the line into the combination should never be shorter than four strides. Remember that combinations in hunter classes generally consist of a vertical to an ascending oxer (square oxers are illegal) or two vertical elements.

COURSE COMPOSITION	
10	Total Number of Obstacles
5	Total Number of Verticals
5	Total Number of Oxers
10	Wing Standards (pairs)
5	Schooling Standards (pairs)
10	Filler Items
25	Poles (less if fillers are used)
10	Ground Lines or Flower Boxes
50	Jump Cups

HUNTER DERBY COURSE 1

NOTES: This is a technical course. Make the distance between the option fences #7 and #8 as long as available space allows.

COURSE COMPOSITION	
12	Total Number of Obstacles
5	Total Number of Verticals
7	Total Number of Oxers
12	Wing Standards (pairs)
7	Schooling Standards (pairs)
12	Filler Items
31	Poles (less if fillers are used)
12	Ground Lines or Flower Boxes
62	Jump Cups

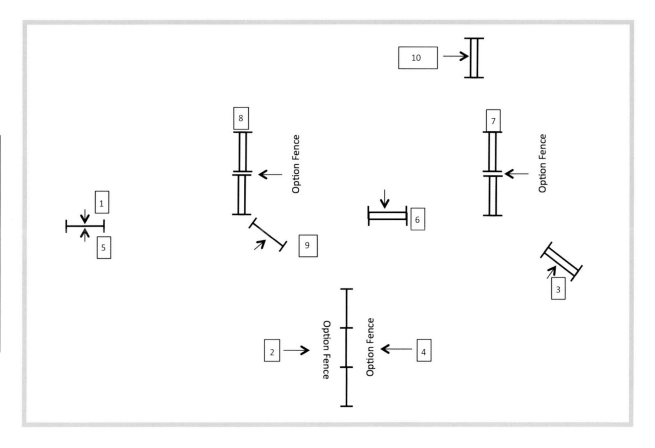

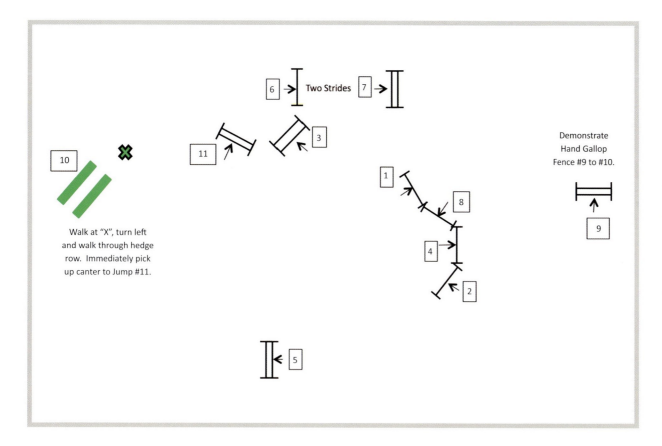

Two Strides (between 6 and 7)

10 — Walk at "X", turn left and walk through hedge row. Immediately pick up canter to Jump #11.

Demonstrate Hand Gallop Fence #9 to #10.

HUNTER DERBY COURSE 2

NOTES: This course has a snake fence (see photo on p. 125). A snake fence is a great way to conserve space in your arena. You should be able to jump all the elements in a snake fence from both directions so you have options for schooling. I also included a walk-through in this course, using hedges, but for practice you can use poles or standing filler, such as two flower boxes. It is good to practice walk-throughs because it is an element that horses can find "spooky" on course. The turn from the walk-through to Fence #11 can be as tight as the rider wants to ride it. The "test" here is the reestablishment of the canter from a walk directly to a spread fence (an oxer) at the end of the course.

COURSE COMPOSITION	
10	Total Number of Obstacles
5	Total Number of Verticals
5	Total Number of Oxers
10	Wing Standards (pairs)
5	Schooling Standards (pairs)
10	Filler Items
25	Poles (less if fillers are used)
10	Ground Lines or Flower Boxes
50	Jump Cups

HUNTER DERBY COURSE 3

NOTES: This course has option fences (Fence #5 and #9—see photos on p. 125). They need to be set so both fences can be jumped in either direction. Because you cannot use square oxers in a hunter class, the options should be something like hedges, brush boxes, roll tops, or walls. You might want to make the two ascending oxers (Fence #4 and #10) somewhat "airy" for contrast to Fence #5 and #9. There is a broken line from Fence #4 to #5 and a bending line when you come back in the other direction, going from Fence #9 to #10.

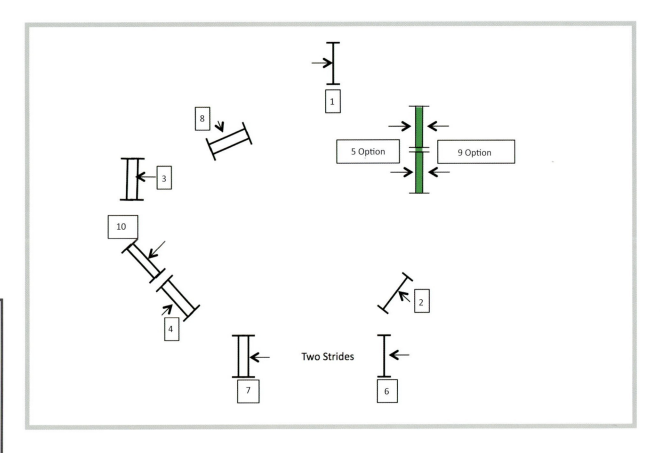

COURSE COMPOSITION	
10	Total Number of Obstacles
5	Total Number of Verticals
5	Total Number of Oxers
10	Wing Standards (pairs)
5	Schooling Standards (pairs)
10	Filler Items
25	Poles (less if fillers are used)
10	Ground Lines or Flower Boxes
50	Jump Cups

EQUITATION COURSES

Equitation courses emphasize the rider's position, form, control, coordination, and effectiveness. Many of the "Medal" or "Talent Search" classes in the equitation divisions are intended as preparation for advancement to the jumper ring or toward a professional career as a hunter rider (and it is these classes that have inspired some of the courses I've provided in the section ahead). Equitation courses incorporate technical elements, such as tight turns and rollbacks, bending and broken lines with optional striding, long gallops, and unrelated distances. Classes usually include a flat phase where the rider's abilities are tested in the ring without jumps. The flat phase is judged subjectively on the rider's body position, use of the aids, and ability to perform basic dressage movements. It is common for riders in equitation classes to be tested without stirrups, both on the flat and over fences.

Equitation courses can include any of the elements found in both the hunter and jumper rings. Equitation over fences and Medal classes usually have hunter-type ("natural") fences, whereas Talent Search classes and some of the equitation classics have fences more typical of those seen in the jumper ring. In fact, some of the equitation classics have

PHOTO COURTESY JAMEE HAINES (2005)

In equitation classes the rider's position and effectiveness is judged. This pair exhibit appropriate turnout for competition.

both a hunter phase and a jumper phase, and the USEF Talent Search class has three parts, including a hunter, jumper, and gymnastic phase.

Equitation classes can require a course walk without the help of a trainer, so it is important to learn to "walk" a course and to understand the questions that it asks (see p. 66 for more on course-walking).

> Attractive fences from a pony equitation class.

USEF TESTS 1-19	
TEST NUMBER	**DESCRIPTION**
1	Halt and/or Back
2	Hand Gallop
3	Figure eight at a trot demonstrating a change of diagonals
4	Figure eight at a canter on the correct lead demonstrating a simple change of lead
5	Collective work at a walk, trot and/or canter
6	Jumping low obstacles at a trot and/or canter
7	Jumping obstacles on a figure eight course
8	Questions regarding horsemanship, tack and equipment, and conformation
9	Riding without stirrups
10	Jumping low obstacles at a walk and canter
11	Dismounting and mounting individually
12	Turn on the forehand
13	Figure eight at canter on the correct lead demonstrating a flying change of lead
14	Serpentine at a trot or a canter demonstrating a simple or flying change of lead
15	Changing leads on a straight line demonstrating a simple or flying change of lead
16	Changing horses
17	Cantering on the counter lead
18	Turn on the haunches
19	Demonstration ride of one minute

This trot fence is a nicely decorated obstacle from an equitation class. When using straw bales as part of your course, be sure that they are tightly bound, and it is best if you include a pole over the top, supported by standards. Straw bales deteriorate quickly, so plan to remove them from your course as soon as they may become a hazard or an eyesore.

An ascending, hunter-type oxer from an equitation course. Note how the beige poles and standards blend into the color of the footing. The greenery and white flowers help draw the focal point to the jump—otherwise, it would be somewhat hard to see.

▲ This coop is made on a 2- by 4-inch triangular frame and faced with cedar planks. Coops are a very traditional hunter-type fence, and often used in the equitation ring. Note how the color of this jump blends in with the footing. Using a darker stain or some additional greenery would make this jump more appealing. Note that USEF/USHJA rules prohibit the use of coops that are only hinged at the top and left unsupported at the bottom. A coop needs to have a support brace across the bottom for stability, so if a horse hits it, it won't collapse. This one has corner support brackets and both lower and middle braces. There are also small metal brackets on the inside supporting the angle at the top of the coop.

COURSE DESIGN CONSIDERATIONS FOR ADVANCED EQUITATION AND MEDAL CLASSES

In advanced equitation, open equitation, and special equitation classes (often referred to as "Medal" classes) the courses become exceedingly difficult. As already mentioned, jumps in these classes can resemble those found on a hunter course, or the course may include jumper-type obstacles that are somewhat conservative in design. The height and spread of the jumps become more challenging: heights range from 3-foot-6-inches to 3-foot-9-inches high, and spreads are up to 4 feet in most cases, with triple bars allowed the maximum of 5 feet in width.

Each advanced course must include at least one change of lead (some require at least two changes after the first fence) and a combination including an oxer. In addition, at least one-third of the obstacles must be oxers. The course must include at least three of the following: a bending line; a narrow ("skinny") jump (6- to 8-feet wide); a rollback turn; a fence at the end of the ring; and a long approach to a single jump.

V An equitation course that features both hunter- and jumper-type fences.

> A narrow or "skinny" jump is frequently included in an equitation class. In an equitation class, "skinnies" can be as narrow as 6 feet. The jump in A (with the stone wall) is 6-and-a-half-feet wide. The post-and-rail "skinny line" in B is 8 feet wide. A skinny jump demonstrates the rider's ability to navigate a straight line. The narrower the fence(s), the more accurate the track has to be.

A

B

> Using option fences in schooling is a great way to practice the different skills needed to ride jumps set at various heights in the equitation ring. These adorable "pig" elements (gate and planks), slanted wings, and schooling standards are from Hi-Tech Horse Jumps (www.hitechhorse-jumps.com). I don't always put out ground lines when I set a course in order to save extra wear and tear on the poles. I will add them during a schooling session.

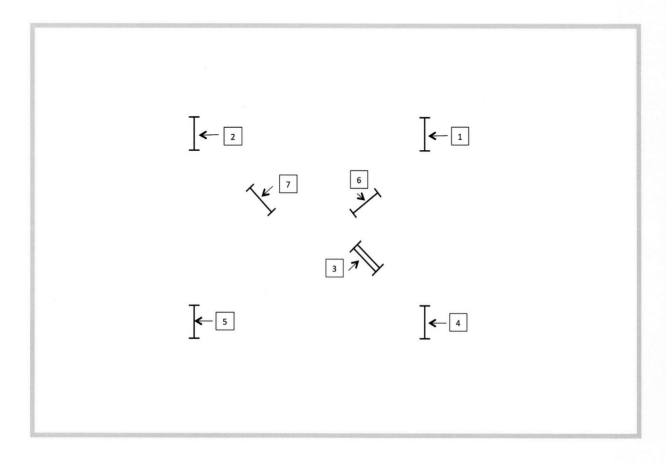

BEGINNER EQUITATION COURSE 1

NOTES: In beginner equitation courses, fences should not exceed 3 feet. One lead change is required. This course starts on a line and has a single oxer set on the diagonal. Otherwise, it is straightforward. (Oxers and combinations are not required at this level.)

COURSE COMPOSITION	
7	Total Number of Obstacles
6	Total Number of Verticals
1	Total Number of Oxers
7	Wing Standards (pairs)
1	Schooling Standards (pairs)
7	Filler Items
15	Poles (less if fillers are used)
7	Ground Lines or Flower Boxes
30	Jump Cups

Note: Square and rectangular outlines in these diagrams do not accurately represent the arena boundary. When setting the exercises in this section, make sure there is room for a safe approach to and landing from each fence, as well as space for turns between obstacles and the fence line or wall.

BEGINNER EQUITATION COURSE 2

NOTES: This course starts with a fence that is jumped out of a line and introduces the kind of slight bending line that riders will often encounter as they move up the levels in equitation.

COURSE COMPOSITION	
8	Total Number of Obstacles
4	Total Number of Verticals
4	Total Number of Oxers
8	Wing Standards (pairs)
4	Schooling Standards (pairs)
8	Filler Items
20	Poles (less if fillers are used)
8	Ground Lines or Flower Boxes
40	Jump Cups

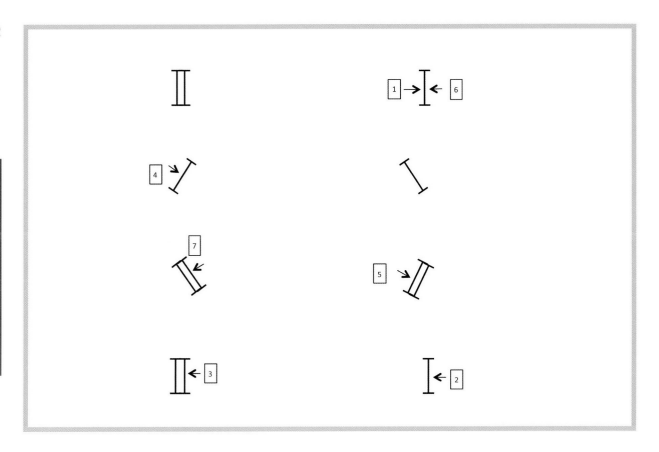

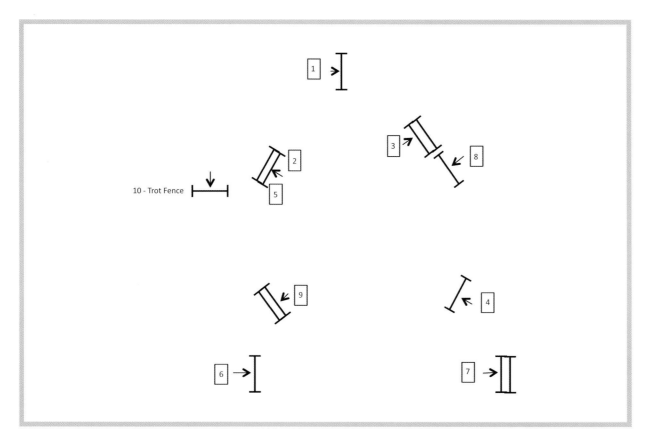

10 - Trot Fence

BEGINNER EQUITATION COURSE 3

NOTES: This course is fairly straightforward; however, a challenge lies in the fact that it ends with a trot fence. Trot fences are fairly common in equitation classes. Set the line from Fence #3 to #4 one stride shorter than the line from Fence #7 to #8.

COURSE COMPOSITION	
9	Total Number of Obstacles
5	Total Number of Verticals
4	Total Number of Oxers
9	Wing Standards (pairs)
4	Schooling Standards (pairs)
9	Filler Items
22	Poles (less if fillers are used)
9	Ground Lines or Flower Boxes
44	Jump Cups

BASIC EQUITATION COURSE 1

NOTES: Basic equitation courses feature fences between 3-foot and 3-foot-3-inches high. They must include at least one change of direction and one combination that includes an oxer, which this course introduces. Per USEF rules, combinations in an equitation class must be numbered with a single number and the designations of "a" and "b," or "a," "b," and "c" on the course diagram.

COURSE COMPOSITION	
9	Total Number of Obstacles
5	Total Number of Verticals
4	Total Number of Oxers
9	Wing Standards (pairs)
4	Schooling Standards (pairs)
9	Filler Items
22	Poles (less if fillers are used)
9	Ground Lines or Flower Boxes
44	Jump Cups

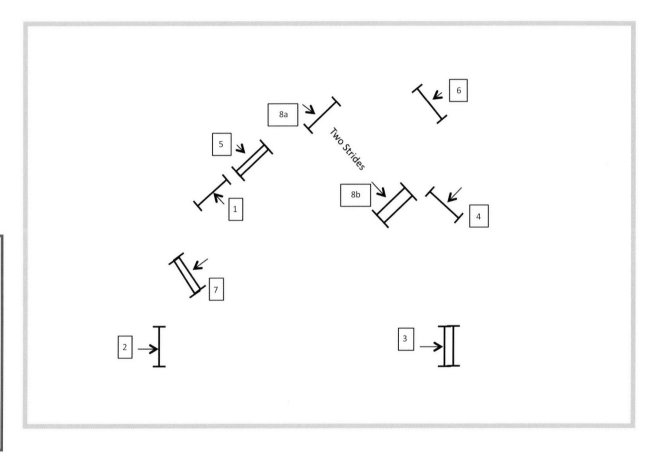

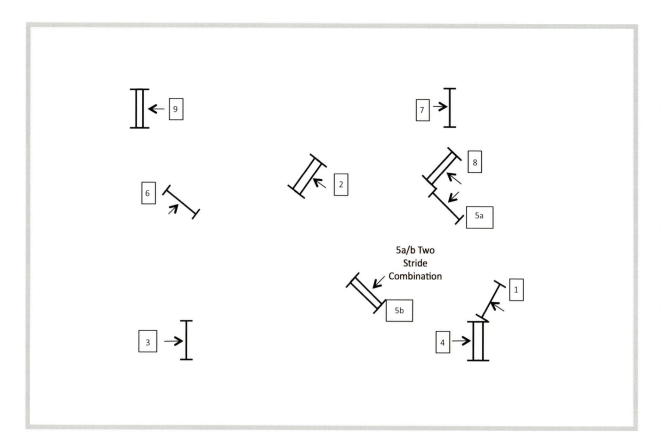

BASIC EQUITATION COURSE 2

NOTES: This course starts on a diagonal line out of a short corner. There is a bending line from Fence #6 to #7 and a broken line from Fence #8 to #9.

COURSE COMPOSITION	
10	Total Number of Obstacles
5	Total Number of Verticals
5	Total Number of Oxers
10	Wing Standards (pairs)
5	Schooling Standards (pairs)
10	Filler Items
25	Poles (less if fillers are used)
10	Ground Lines or Flower Boxes
50	Jump Cups

5a/b Two
Stride
Combination

BASIC EQUITATION COURSE 3

NOTES: This course has a number of turns with relatively tight angles. It has a bending line from Fence #5 to the #6 a/b combination, and a rollback turn from Fence #7 back to Fence #8.

COURSE COMPOSITION	
9	Total Number of Obstacles
4	Total Number of Verticals
5	Total Number of Oxers
9	Wing Standards (pairs)
5	Schooling Standards (pairs)
9	Filler Items
23	Poles (less if fillers are used)
9	Ground Lines or Flower Boxes
46	Jump Cups

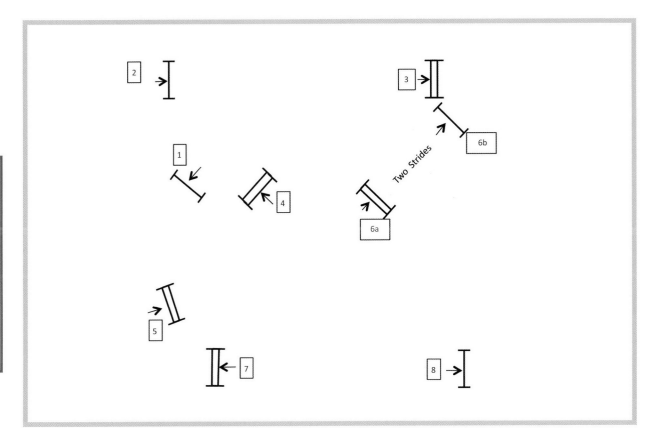

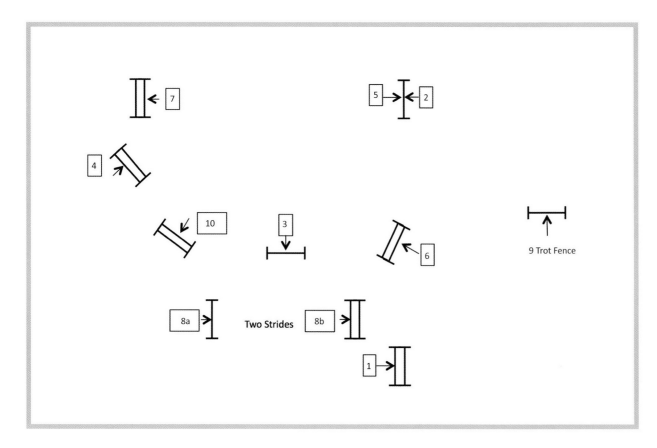

9 Trot Fence

Two Strides

INTERMEDIATE EQUITATION COURSE 1

NOTES: Intermediate equitation courses feature fences between 3-foot-3-inches and 3-foot-6-inches high. They must include at least one change of direction and one combination that involves an oxer. In this example, the "test" from the trot fence to Fence #10 is the reestablishment of the canter. It will be more easily achieved when the direction of Fence #10 is toward the in-gate.

COURSE COMPOSITION	
10	Total Number of Obstacles
4	Total Number of Verticals
6	Total Number of Oxers
10	Wing Standards (pairs)
6	Schooling Standards (pairs)
10	Filler Items
26	Poles (less if fillers are used)
10	Ground Lines or Flower Boxes
52	Jump Cups

INTERMEDIATE EQUITATION COURSE 2

NOTES: This course has a figure-eight track from Fence #2 to #3 (a half-turn in reverse). Otherwise, it is a fairly straightforward, hunter-type course.

COURSE COMPOSITION	
11	Total Number of Obstacles
6	Total Number of Verticals
5	Total Number of Oxers
11	Wing Standards (pairs)
5	Schooling Standards (pairs)
11	Filler Items
27	Poles (less if fillers are used)
11	Ground Lines or Flower Boxes
54	Jump Cups

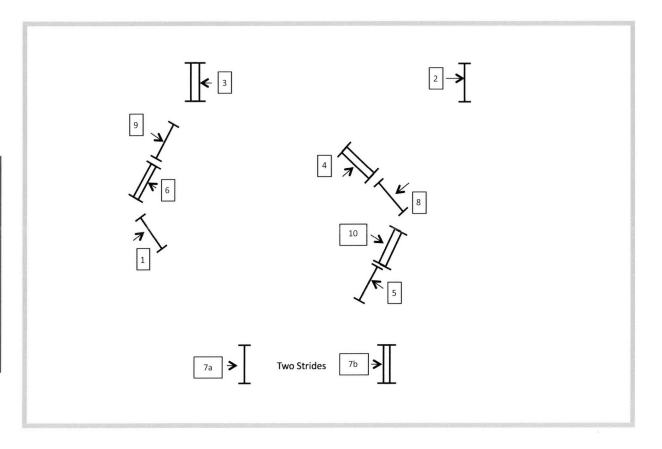

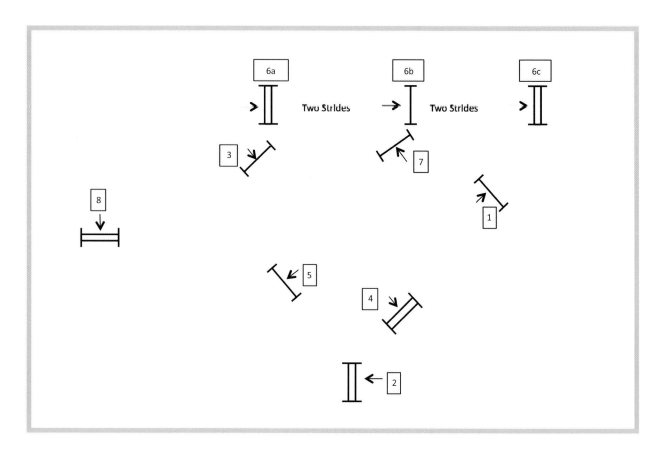

INTERMEDIATE EQUITATION COURSE 3

NOTES: This is more of a jumper-type course, with a rollback turn from Fence #4 to #5, a triple combination, and an end fence (#8). Make sure that you leave enough room between the triple combination and the rail (at least 8 feet, and 10 to 12 feet is preferable) so that you have adequate room to travel away from Fence #7.

COURSE COMPOSITION	
10	Total Number of Obstacles
5	Total Number of Verticals
5	Total Number of Oxers
10	Wing Standards (pairs)
5	Schooling Standards (pairs)
10	Filler Items
25	Poles (less if fillers are used)
10	Ground Lines or Flower Boxes
50	Jump Cups

INTERMEDIATE EQUITATION COURSE 4

NOTES: This equitation course has a jumper emphasis and begins with a line rather than a single fence. It includes a triple combination that you would commonly see in a jumper class, especially because the first element in the combination is an oxer. Set Fence #6 so that you have room to take a track to either the inside or outside of it.

COURSE COMPOSITION	
10	Total Number of Obstacles
5	Total Number of Verticals
5	Total Number of Oxers
10	Wing Standards (pairs)
5	Schooling Standards (pairs)
10	Filler Items
25	Poles (less if fillers are used)
10	Ground Lines or Flower Boxes
50	Jump Cups

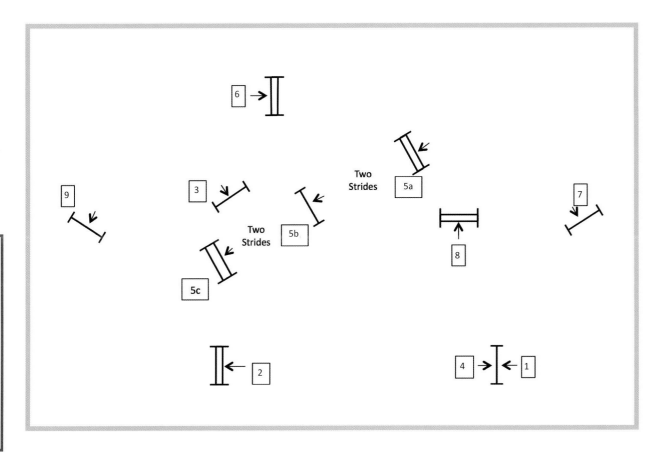

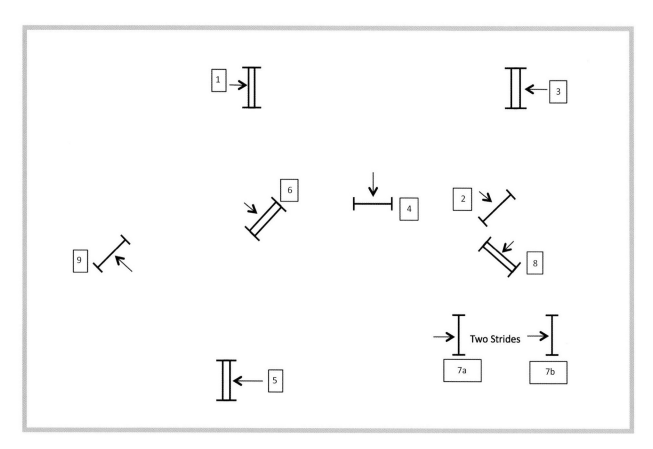

ADVANCED EQUITATION/MEDAL COURSE 1

NOTES: The height of the jumps at the highest level of equitation competition range will be a minimum of 3'6" and/or 3'9" with spreads up to 4 feet (exception: triple bar type obstacles can have a maximum of 5 feet in width). This course has the classic "S" turn between Fences #3, #4, and #5. There is a short bending line between Fence #6 and #7a/b, with a tight rollback to Fence #8. The final two fences form a broken line with a lead change between Fences #8 and #9.

COURSE COMPOSITION	
10	Total Number of Obstacles
5	Total Number of Verticals
5	Total Number of Oxers
10	Wing Standards (pairs)
5	Schooling Standards (pairs)
10	Filler Items
25	Poles (less if fillers are used)
10	Ground Lines or Flower Boxes
50	Jump Cups

ADVANCED EQUITATION/MEDAL COURSE 2

NOTES: This course has a number of difficult tests. The broken line back to the final combination of 9a/b is especially difficult, as is the combination itself. Similar elements have been used in several of the Maclay Finals, and often after jumping the 9a/b combination, the course routes you back through it, going the opposite direction. In addition, the course finishes on a skinny jump (see p. 146 for photos).

COURSE COMPOSITION	
11	Total Number of Obstacles
6	Total Number of Verticals
5	Total Number of Oxers
11	Wing Standards (pairs)
5	Schooling Standards (pairs)
11	Filler Items
27	Poles (less if fillers are used)
11	Ground Lines or Flower Boxes
54	Jump Cups

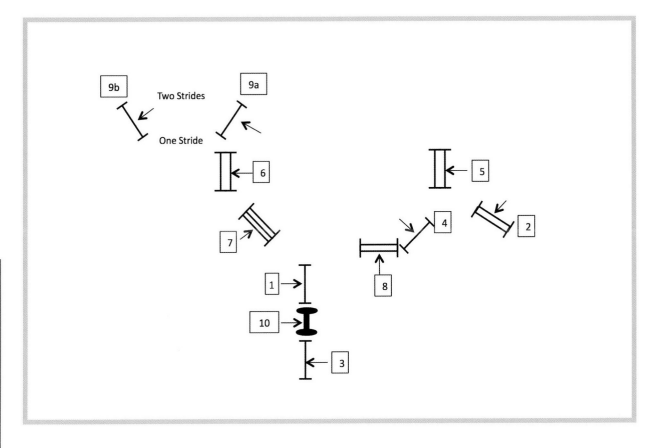

Two Strides

One Stride

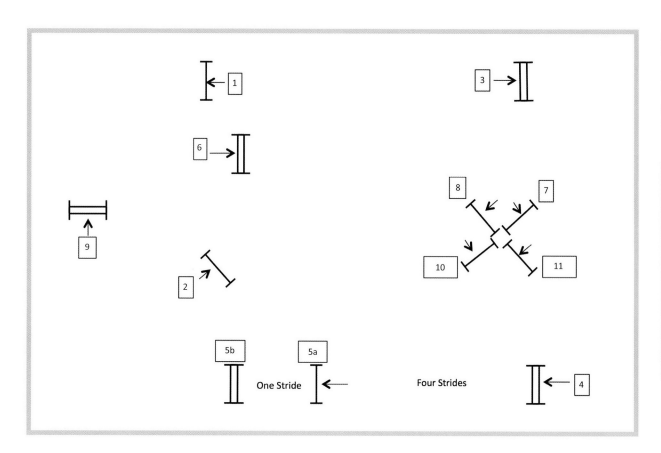

ADVANCED EQUITATION/MEDAL COURSE 3

NOTES: The pinwheel (see p. 97) featured in this course challenges the rider to perform well-planned bending lines and rollback turns.

COURSE COMPOSITION	
12	Total Number of Obstacles
7	Total Number of Verticals
5	Total Number of Oxers
12	Wing Standards (pairs)
5	Schooling Standards (pairs)
12	Filler Items
29	Poles (less if fillers are used)
12	Ground Lines or Flower Boxes
58	Jump Cups

One Stride

Four Strides

ADVANCED EQUITATION/MEDAL COURSE 4

NOTES: When you have a small arena it can be hard to fit a line with three obstacles, so be careful that you set this course so you have enough room to get to the combination #7 a/b and land and turn at the end of the line after Fence #8. You could end after Fence #10, but as drawn, this course allows you a final long gallop to the last line, which includes jumping the Liverpool from the opposite direction than it was ridden earlier in the course.

COURSE COMPOSITION	
11	Total Number of Obstacles
5	Total Number of Verticals
6	Total Number of Oxers
11	Wing Standards (pairs)
6	Schooling Standards (pairs)
9	Filler Items
28	Poles (less if fillers are used)
11	Ground Lines or Flower Boxes
56	Jump Cups

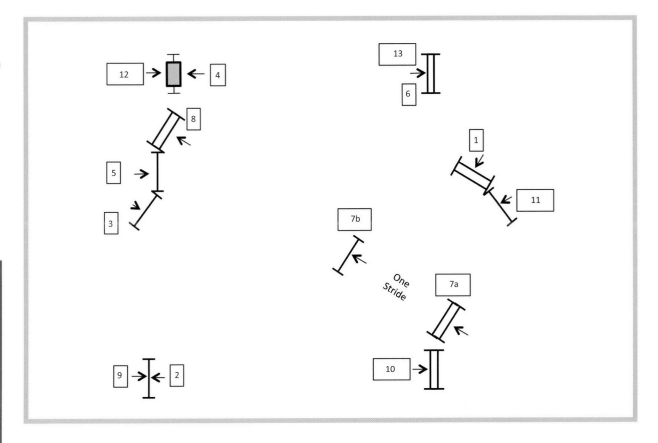

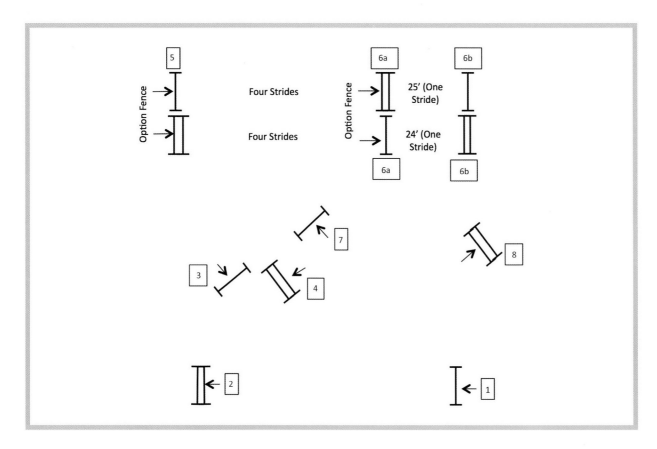

ADVANCED EQUITATION/MEDAL COURSE 5

NOTES: This course starts on a line and there is a tight rollback turn from Fence #2 to #3 and from Fence #3 to #4 (although you could go around Fence #8 on the way to #4 to make the turn easier). The optional lines for Fences #5 to #6 test the rider's ability to ride either a vertical to an oxer and an oxer to a vertical. When you take the oxer/vertical/oxer line the four strides will ride a little long and the in-and-out will ride a little short. When you take the vertical/oxer/vertical line, the four strides will ride a little short and the in-and-out will ride longer.

COURSE COMPOSITION	
12	Total Number of Obstacles
6	Total Number of Verticals
8	Total Number of Oxers
12	Wing Standards (pairs)
6	Schooling Standards (pairs)
12	Filler Items
30	Poles (less if fillers are used)
12	Ground Lines or Flower Boxes
60	Jump Cups

ADVANCED GYMNASTIC COURSES

In chapter 6 I introduced you to some basic gymnastic exercises, which aim to develop strength and agility in both horse and rider, and emphasize basic riding skills, such as maintaining rhythm, varying stride length, improving adjustability, and balancing turns. This section takes gymnastics to a new level—it combines them into a course. Putting all the skills required in multiple gymnastic exercises into a single series of "tests" is highly technical and should only be used by advanced riders. It requires riders be prompt and crystal clear in the execution of cues and aids.

Obstacles in a gymnastics course, just like in individual gymnastic exercises, should be kept simple without a lot of fill so they are easily moved and adjusted. Gymnastic courses can include gait transitions before or in a line, turns, and frequently incorporate grids (see p. 70). Gymnastic Courses 1 and Gymnastic Course 2 (pp. 166 and 167) were inspired by Bertalan de Némethy's gymnastic courses included in his book *The de Némethy Method* (Doubleday, 1988). The remaining gymnastic courses in

> Examples from three advanced gymnastic courses used for schooling at my farm.

A horse and rider schooling over a gymnastic course.

PHOTO COURTESY BETH CAHILL

A

B

this section are examples of what you might see in the gymnastic phases of a Medal or Talent Search class, and they are quite technical. All of these courses can be made simpler by using only poles on the ground, straightening the lines, lengthening the distance between elements in the grids/combinations, and/or incorporating more flatwork and gait transitions.

Photo A shows a gymnastic course that I use inside. It involves several different cavalletti exercises. In B you can see the different types of risers that I use—longeing standards with jump cups support the blue pole in back. The PVC risers in the foreground are from JumPVC (18-inch and 24-inch heights). They are easy to lift, move, and store.

A typical grid or combination used in gymnastic courses.

Advanced Gymnastic Courses

ADVANCED GYMNASTIC COURSE 1

NOTES: I like to use this course from Bertalan de Némethy's book *The de Némethy Method: Modern Techniques for Training the Show Jumper and Its Rider.* (You can find it in its original form in that book's Appendix 21.)

COURSE COMPOSITION	
12	Total Number of Obstacles
3	Total Number of Verticals
9	Total Number of Oxers
12	Wing Standards (pairs)
9	Schooling Standards (pairs)
12	Filler Items
33	Poles (less if fillers are used)
12	Ground Lines or Flower Boxes
66	Jump Cups

Note: Square and rectangular outlines in these diagrams do not accurately represent the arena boundary. When setting the exercises in this section, make sure there is room for a safe approach to and landing from each fence, as well as space for turns between obstacles and the fence line or wall.

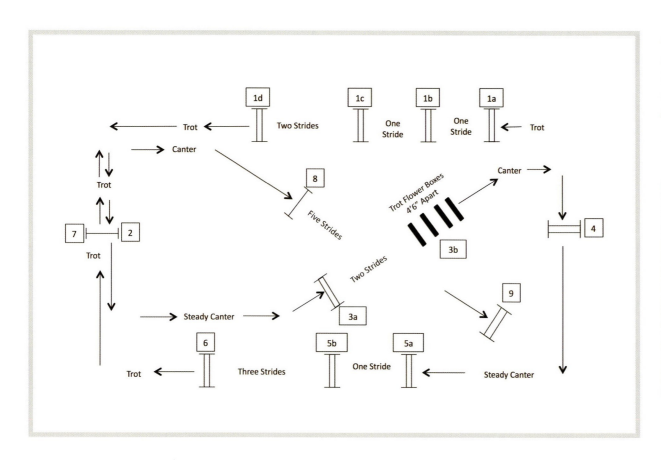

ADVANCED GYMNASTIC COURSE 2

NOTES: I also use this course, again from Bertalan de Némethy's book *The de Némethy Method: Modern Techniques for Training the Show Jumper and Its Rider*. (You can find it in its original form in that book's Appendix 22.)

COURSE COMPOSITION	
12	Total Number of Obstacles
2	Total Number of Verticals
10	Total Number of Oxers
12	Wing Standards (pairs)
10	Schooling Standards (pairs)
12	Filler Items
34	Poles (less if fillers are used)
16	Ground Lines or Flower Boxes
68	Jump Cups

ADVANCED GYMNASTIC COURSE 3

NOTES: This is a valuable basic gymnastic course, as once you have it set up, you have many options for practicing variations in stride length. (Refer to the section on distances, p. 21, and the one on grids, p. 70, for more information on determining distances.) The grids set in the middle of the arena help you practice how an oxer to vertical, vertical to oxer line can ride. The track between Fence #1 and #2 and Fence #5 and #6 can be straight, bending, or broken. Using a 60-foot distance between the elements allows for a choice in the number of strides to be ridden: four, five, or six.

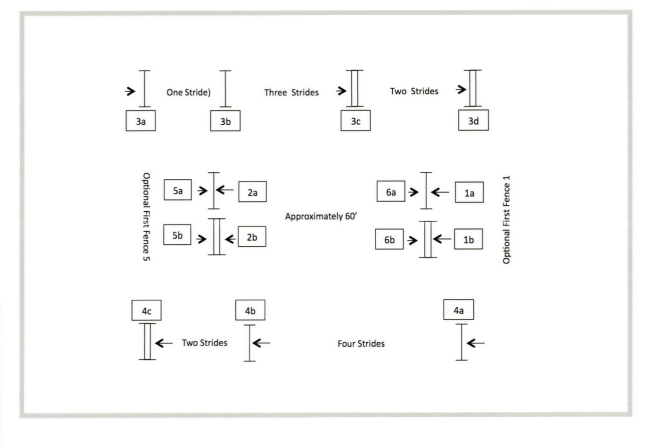

COURSE COMPOSITION	
11	Total Number of Obstacles
6	Total Number of Verticals
5	Total Number of Oxers
11	Wing Standards (pairs)
5	Schooling Standards (pairs)
11	Filler Items
27	Poles (less if fillers are used)
15	Ground Lines or Flower Boxes
54	Jump Cups

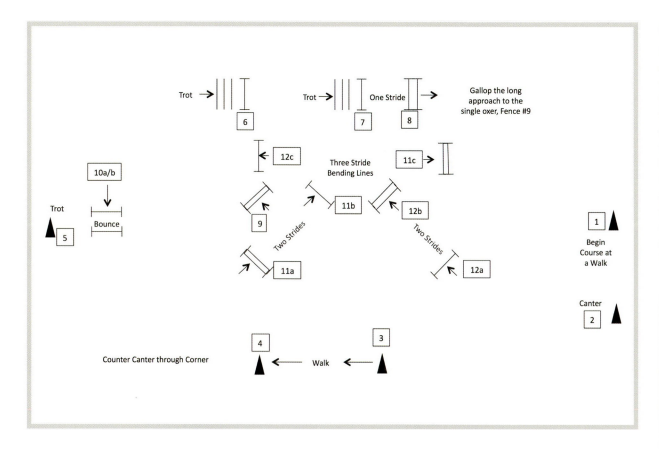

ADVANCED GYMNASTIC COURSE 4

NOTES: The objective of a gymnastic course is to show an understanding of the bridge between flatwork and jumping. Therefore, gymnastic courses include flatwork elements, such as counter-canter, simple or flying lead changes, gait transitions, quick turns, and shortening and lengthening of stride. These flatwork elements are evident in this course. Both the #11 a/b/c and the #12 a/b/c combinations are very technical. Not only is the distance between the elements very close, both combinations incorporate a bending line that is only three strides.

COURSE COMPOSITION	
12	Total Number of Obstacles
7	Total Number of Verticals
5	Total Number of Oxers
12	Wing Standards (pairs)
5	Schooling Standards (pairs)
12	Filler Items
29	Poles (less if fillers are used)
18	Ground Lines or Flower Boxes
58	Jump Cups

ADVANCED GYMNASTIC COURSE 5

NOTES: Each element that is set in a gymnastic course should have a purpose, requiring the rider to demonstrate a specific, definable skill. Flying lead changes, bending or broken lines, and at least one long gallop to a single fence should be included.

COURSE COMPOSITION	
12	Total Number of Obstacles
7	Total Number of Verticals
5	Total Number of Oxers
12	Wing Standards (pairs)
5	Schooling Standards (pairs)
12	Filler Items
29	Poles (less if fillers are used)
15	Ground Lines or Flower Boxes
58	Jump Cups

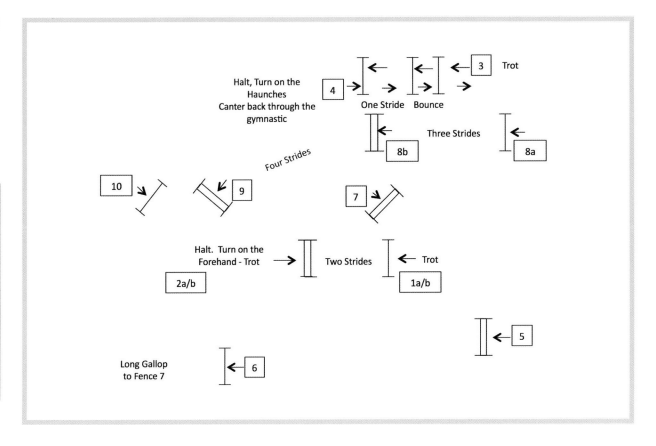

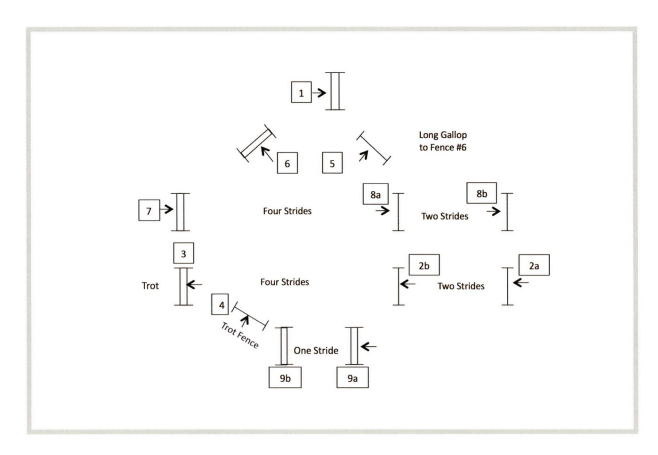

Long Gallop to Fence #6

Four Strides

Four Strides

Trot

Trot Fence

One Stride

ADVANCED GYMNASTIC COURSE 6

NOTES: When setting a gymnastic course, include some fences and lines where the stride needs to be compressed (collected), and some fences and lines that will be approached at a strong gallop (lengthened). The more you alter, or alternate, the change in pace/impulsion, the more technical the course is. In this example, the #2a/b to #3, and the #7 to #8a/b combination lines are set identically, but one is a combination to a line, the other is a line to a combination. Fence # 5 and #6 could also be used as bending line elements (#7 to #5 or #2a/b to #6, for example).

COURSE COMPOSITION	
12	Total Number of Obstacles
6	Total Number of Verticals
6	Total Number of Oxers
12	Wing Standards (pairs)
6	Schooling Standards (pairs)
12	Filler Items
30	Poles (less if fillers are used)
12	Ground Lines or Flower Boxes
60	Jump Cups

ADVANCED GYMNASTIC COURSE 7

NOTES: Keep in mind that the "tests" in a gymnastic course come up quickly, and you need to have adequate room to get to, and land from, all the elements that you set. Because most of these advanced gymnastic courses have a lot of elements, you will probably have to set many of the grids and lines on the rail or horizontally across the ring to give you more room through the middle of the arena for changes of direction.

COURSE COMPOSITION	
14	Total Number of Obstacles
8	Total Number of Verticals
6	Total Number of Oxers
14	Wing Standards (pairs)
6	Schooling Standards (pairs)
14	Filler Items
34	Poles (less if fillers are used)
14	Ground Lines or Flower Boxes
68	Jump Cups

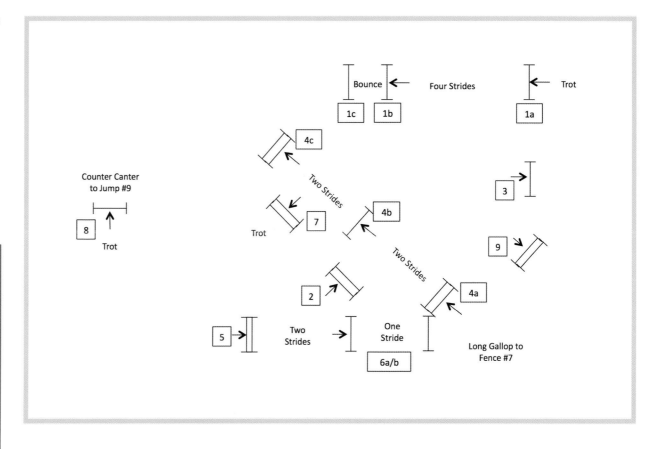

A jumper course, which emphasizes the speed and agility of the horse.

JUMPER COURSES

Jumper courses emphasize the speed and agility of the horse. They are the most technical courses in terms of track, as there are often several options for approaching each fence or striding within a line. These courses require the ability to adjust stride length and an understanding of the optimum pace needed to complete the course in the time required, without knocking any of the jumps down.

Jumper classes are won by the horse-and-rider combination that has the least number of faults/penalties with the fastest time. Faults are incurred for a number of reasons: knocking an element down, refusing/running-out, or failure to complete the course in an allotted time. These classes can be scored in a number of ways under

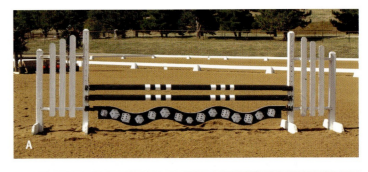

V A colorful vertical from the pony jumper ring.

∧ Here are different configurations for setting poles and planks on jumper fences—all of which are acceptable. Any "wavy" filler component should have a pole above it to serve as the top of the jump. In fact, planks in general should be "topped" by a pole. In some jumper classes, planks are set as the top rail in flat cups so that the slightest touch will cause them to fall. The wavy dice planks are from Hi-Tech Horse Jumps (www.hitechhorsejumps.com).

USEF rules, depending upon the *Jumper Table*, which defines how the class is to be conducted. The specific "table" used is designated in the prize list of every horse show: *Table II* courses are scored (placed) based on faults and time; *Table III* courses are scored by converting faults into time penalties; *Table IV* courses are scored first on faults and then on the competitor that completes the course closest to the *Optimum Time* (usually four seconds less that the allotted time to complete the course).

Every jumper course must have a minimum of 10 jumping efforts, at least three spread fences in the first eight obstacles, and at least one combination. Course

FENCE HEIGHT EQUIVALENTS			
METERS	**FEET/INCHES**	**METERS**	**FEET/INCHES**
0.70 m	2'3"	1.20 m	3'11"
0.75 m	2'5"	1.25 m	4'1"
0.80 m	2'7"	1.30 m	4'3"
0.85 m	2'9"	1.35 m	4'5"
0.90 m	2'11"	1.40 m	4'7"
0.95 m	3'1"	1.45 m	4'9"
1.00 m	3'3"	1.50 m	4'11"
1.05 m	3'5"	1.55 m	5'1"
1.10 m	3'7"	1.60 m	5'3"
1.15 m	3'9"	1.65 m	5'5"

< Jumper fence height equivalents in metric and English units.

V USHJA jumper levels and associated fence heights.

∧ This kind of hanging filler is often referred to as a "panel" rather than a gate. Solid panels are most often seen in jumper classes, but you see planks or standing hurdles used far more frequently as filler. These colorful jump components are from Hi-Tech Horse Jumps (www.hitechhorsejumps.com).

USHJA JUMPER LEVELS				
USHJA JUMPER LEVELS	**HEIGHT**	**WIDTH**	**TRIPLE BARS and LIVERPOOLS**	**WATER OBSTACLES**
Level 1	2'9" to 3'0"	3'0" to 3'6"	Up to 4'0"	N/A
Level 2	3'0" to 3'3"	3'3" to 3'9"	Up to 4'3"	N/A
Level 3	3'3" to 3'6"	3'6" to 4'0"	Up to 4'6"	N/A
Level 4	3'6" to 3'9"	3'9" to 4'3"	Up to 4'9"	Up to 8'0"
Level 5	3'9" to 4'0"	4'0" to 4'6"	Up to 5'0"	Up to 9'0"
Level 6	4'0" to 4'3"	4'3" to 4'9"	Up to 5'3"	Up to 10'0"
Level 7	4'3" to 4'6"	4'6" to 5'0"	Up to 5'6"	Up to 12'0"
Level 8	4'6" to 4'9"	4'9" to 5'3"	Up to 5'9"	Up to 12'6"
Level 9	4'9" to 5'0"	5'0" to 5'6"	Up to 6'0"	Up to 13'0"

▶ Attractive square oxers from the schooling arena (A) and the jumper ring at a horse show (B & C). Planks and poles as in A and B are the most common components used in jumper courses. Note that pillars are used to frame the jump in C instead of wing standards. The red flag and white flag that designate the direction the fence should be jumped are clearly visible in B and C.

elements include striped rails, brightly colored standards with decorative elements, open airy jumps with poles, substantial walls, water jumps and liverpools, fan jumps, triple bars, banks, planks, and more. It is common to have a jumper course begin with an oxer element or a line, as compared to the single vertical element typically utilized as the first fence in a hunter course.

All the jumper courses I have provided are labeled "intermediate." They are intended for horses and riders jumping heights between 1.00 meters (3'0") up to 1.15 meters (3'9"). Jumper courses and their fence heights are measured in meters; even so, all courses in the pages ahead are drawn in feet and the number of strides between jumps is notated when appropriate. Please see the conversion chart on p. 175 for converting meters to feet as necessary.

GRAND PRIX SHOW JUMPING

Grand Prix is the highest level of show jumping. It is run under the Fédération Equestre Internationale (FEI) rules. In Grand Prix, the horse jumps a course of 10 to 16 obstacles with heights and spreads up to 2 meters (6'5"). Grand Prix show jumping competitions include the Olympics and the World Equestrian Games (WEG), among others.

A Liverpool (water tray) is a common element in jumper classes. Placing a gate over the Liverpool and using ground lines, as shown here, can be useful in schooling as it can make the jump less intimidating to the horse. At a horse show, it is more likely that only a single rail or several rails are set over the Liverpool. If the Liverpool is set so it is in front of the front vertical plane of the fence, the jump will be harder (and wider) than when the poles are directly above it. It is even more difficult when the Liverpool is set behind the front vertical plane; it is one instance where a false ground line (see p. 8) can be used, but it is an advanced placement.

This is a nice "skinny" with a sailing theme from the jumper ring. The jump is approximately 8 feet in width, which is the minimum allowed in jumper classes.

Jumper Courses

INTERMEDIATE JUMPER COURSE 1

NOTES: When setting this course, make sure you have adequate room to get to, and land from, all the jumps, and that you do not have any interference in the track(s). Since you need to go through the middle of the combination (Fence #4a/b) and the middle of the Fence #7 and #8 line to get to other obstacles, these jumps need to be set a minimum of 8 feet (and preferably 10 to 12 feet) off the rail.

COURSE COMPOSITION	
10	Total Number of Obstacles
4	Total Number of Verticals
6	Total Number of Oxers
10	Wing Standards (pairs)
6	Schooling Standards (pairs)
10	Filler Items
26	Poles (less if fillers are used)
10	Ground Lines or Flower Boxes
52	Jump Cups

Note: Square and rectangular outlines in these diagrams do not accurately represent the arena boundary. When setting the exercises in this section, make sure there is room for a safe approach to and landing from each fence, as well as space for turns between obstacles and the fence line or wall.

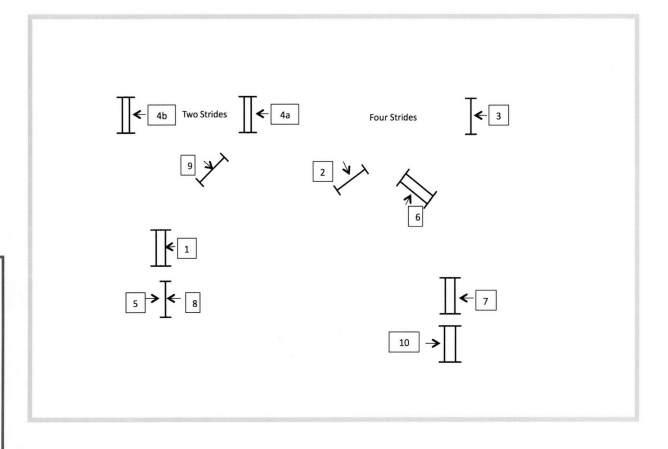

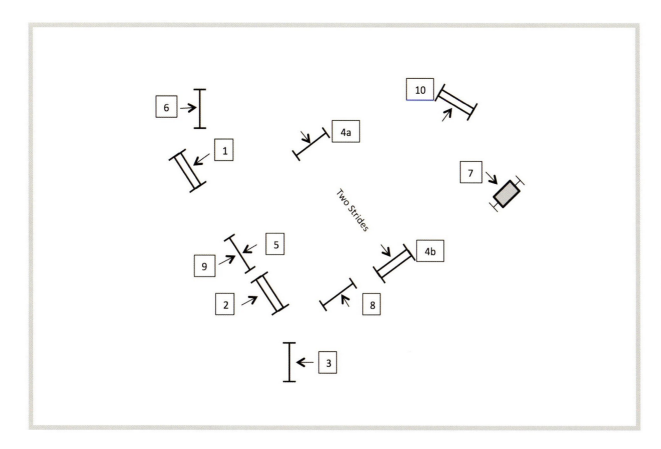

INTERMEDIATE JUMPER COURSE 2

NOTES: This course starts with a roll-back turn from Fence #1 to #2, which will make it more difficult to establish and keep your pace at the beginning. The course includes two bending lines, one off each lead (Fence #6 to #7 and Fence #9 to #10). There is a lot of "crisscrossing" between the tracks, so watch out for track interference when setting the jumps.

COURSE COMPOSITION	
10	Total Number of Obstacles
5	Total Number of Verticals
5	Total Number of Oxers
10	Wing Standards (pairs)
5	Schooling Standards (pairs)
10	Filler Items
25	Poles (less if fillers are used)
10	Ground Lines or Flower Boxes
50	Jump Cups

INTERMEDIATE JUMPER
COURSE 3

NOTES: This course has a number of
broken lines and there are a lot of jumps
in the middle of the ring, so again, watch
for track interference. Also note that the
track from Fence #8 to #9 goes through
the middle of the two-stride combination, taking the horse close to the rail,
so leave enough room to make the turn.

COURSE COMPOSITION	
10	Total Number of Obstacles
5	Total Number of Verticals
5	Total Number of Oxers
10	Wing Standards (pairs)
5	Schooling Standards (pairs)
10	Filler Items
25	Poles (less if fillers are used)
10	Ground Lines or Flower Boxes
50	Jump Cups

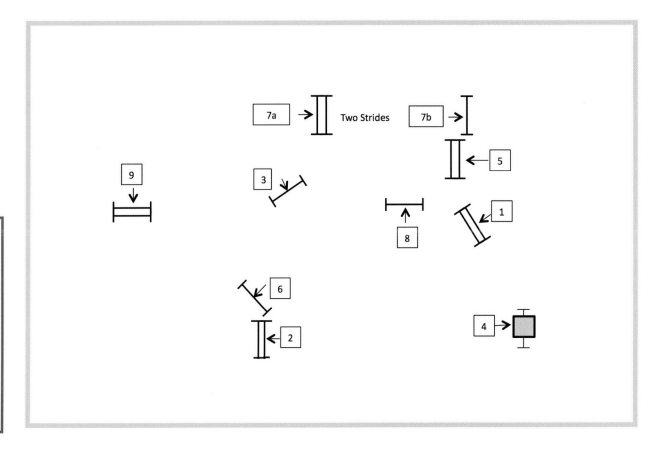

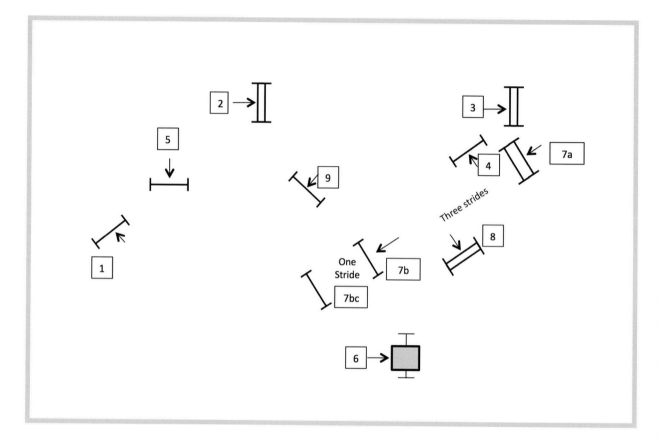

INTERMEDIATE JUMPER COURSE 4

NOTES: When designing a jumper course, avoid putting more than two verticals or two oxers in succession. Ideally, a course should have about the same number of verticals and spreads, and they should be alternated throughout. You should also have approximately the same number of fences to be jumped off each lead. The tracks for both Fence #4 and Fence #8 travel between the three-to-one-stride combination, so be especially aware of your need for space when setting this part of the course.

COURSE COMPOSITION	
11	Total Number of Obstacles
6	Total Number of Verticals
5	Total Number of Oxers
11	Wing Standards (pairs)
5	Schooling Standards (pairs)
11	Filler Items
27	Poles (less if fillers are used)
11	Ground Lines or Flower Boxes
54	Jump Cups

INTERMEDIATE JUMPER
COURSE 5

NOTES: This fairly straightforward course and track allow for a lot of room between jumps. With a few simple modifications (reversal of oxers and verticals where appropriate), this could easily become a hunter or equitation course. Make sure that you set the outside lines at least 8 feet (preferably 10 to 12 feet) off the rail so you have room to travel around the course.

COURSE COMPOSITION	
11	Total Number of Obstacles
5	Total Number of Verticals
6	Total Number of Oxers
11	Wing Standards (pairs)
6	Schooling Standards (pairs)
11	Filler Items
28	Poles (less if fillers are used)
11	Ground Lines or Flower Boxes
56	Jump Cups

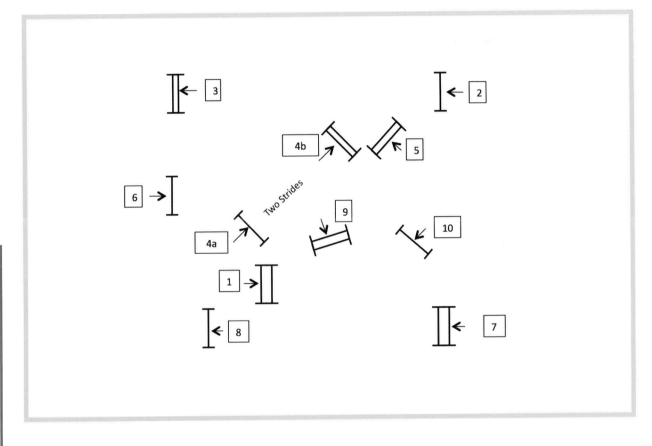

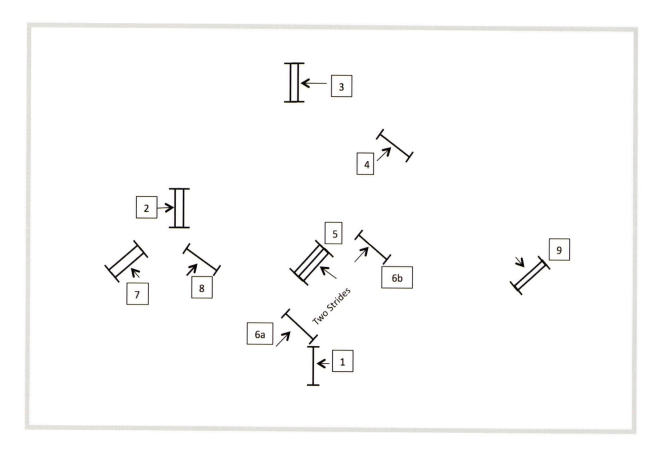

INTERMEDIATE JUMPER COURSE 6

NOTES: This course begins with an "S" turn and is made up of all single fences, with the exception of the combination #6a/b, and has lots of turns. It also introduces a triple bar (Fence #5). As always, watch for track interference when setting this course.

COURSE COMPOSITION	
10	Total Number of Obstacles
5	Total Number of Verticals
5	Total Number of Oxers
10	Wing Standards (pairs)
5	Schooling Standards (pairs)
10	Filler Items
25	Poles (less if fillers are used)
10	Ground Lines or Flower Boxes
50	Jump Cups

INTERMEDIATE JUMPER COURSE 7

NOTES: This is a fun course! It has both bending (Fence #1 to Fence #2) and broken (Fence #5b and Fence #6 and again between Fence #7 and Fence #8) lines.

COURSE COMPOSITION	
11	Total Number of Obstacles
5	Total Number of Verticals
6	Total Number of Oxers
11	Wing Standards (pairs)
6	Schooling Standards (pairs)
11	Filler Items
28	Poles (less if fillers are used)
11	Ground Lines or Flower Boxes
56	Jump Cups

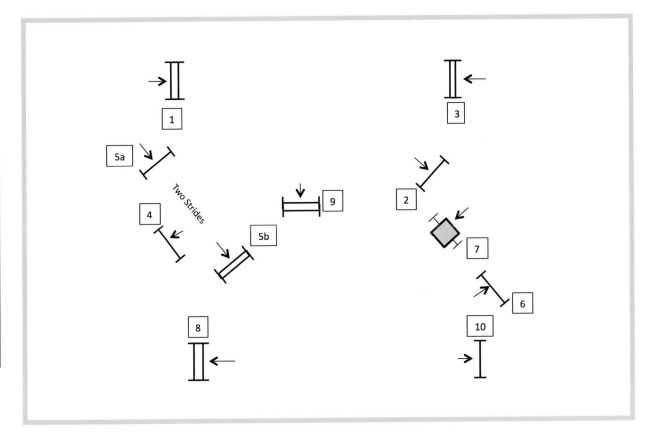

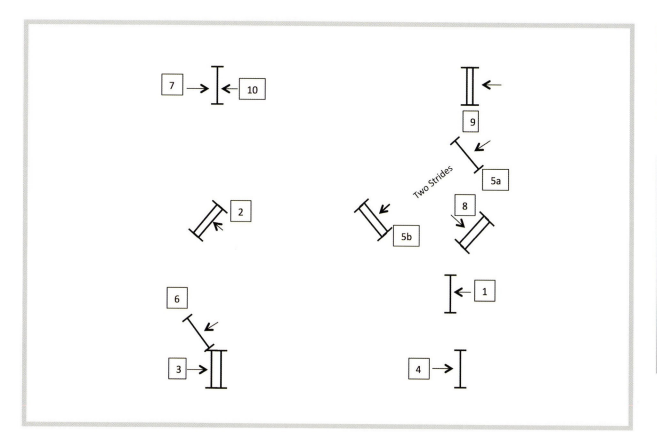

INTERMEDIATE JUMPER COURSE 8

NOTES: This course has a straightforward track that invites the introduction of a new or unusual type of jump, such as a Swedish oxer, a skinny, or a Liverpool.

COURSE COMPOSITION	
10	Total Number of Obstacles
5	Total Number of Verticals
5	Total Number of Oxers
10	Wing Standards (pairs)
5	Schooling Standards (pairs)
10	Filler Items
25	Poles (less if fillers are used)
10	Ground Lines or Flower Boxes
50	Jump Cups

INTERMEDIATE JUMPER COURSE 9

NOTES: This course has two combinations. If your ring is on the small size, it may be difficult to get the two combinations to ride comfortably and still have enough room to maintain appropriate tracks to all the other obstacles, so use discretion. One combination is set off the right lead (#4a/b) and one is off the left lead (#9a/b).

COURSE COMPOSITION	
11	Total Number of Obstacles
5	Total Number of Verticals
6	Total Number of Oxers
11	Wing Standards (pairs)
6	Schooling Standards (pairs)
11	Filler Items
28	Poles (less if fillers are used)
11	Ground Lines or Flower Boxes
56	Jump Cups

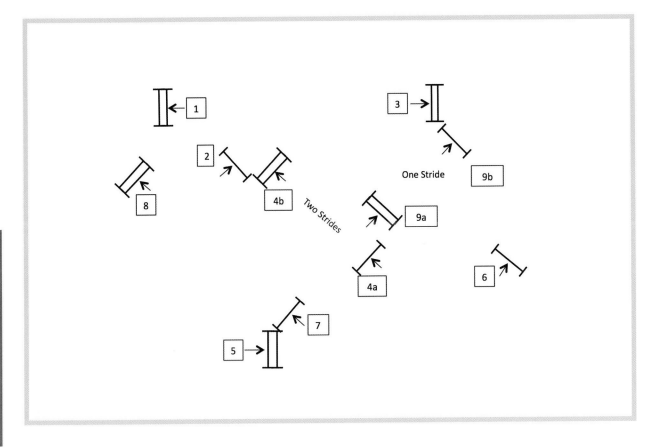

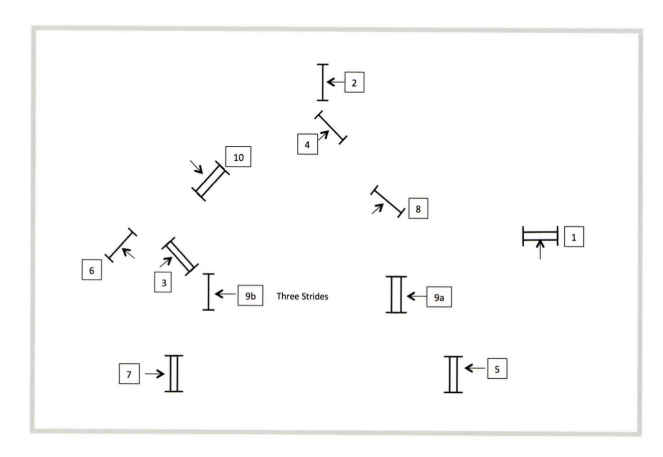

INTERMEDIATE JUMPER COURSE 10

NOTES: This course starts on an end fence. Because it is otherwise straight-forward, consider including different types of fences, such as a skinny, a Swedish oxer, and/or a fan jump, just to make it a little different and add a little challenge.

COURSE COMPOSITION	
11	Total Number of Obstacles
5	Total Number of Verticals
6	Total Number of Oxers
11	Wing Standards (pairs)
6	Schooling Standards (pairs)
11	Filler Items
28	Poles (less if fillers are used)
11	Ground Lines or Flower Boxes
56	Jump Cups

Three Strides

INTERMEDIATE JUMPER COURSE 11

NOTES: You can make this course more challenging by altering the distances in the line to the combination (#5 to #6a/b). If you have space constraints, you can alter the configuration to a triple combination, as opposed to a line to a double. Refer to the recommended guidelines for distances in combinations on p. 26.

COURSE COMPOSITION	
10	Total Number of Obstacles
5	Total Number of Verticals
5	Total Number of Oxers
10	Wing Standards (pairs)
5	Schooling Standards (pairs)
10	Filler Items
25	Poles (less if fillers are used)
10	Ground Lines or Flower Boxes
50	Jump Cups

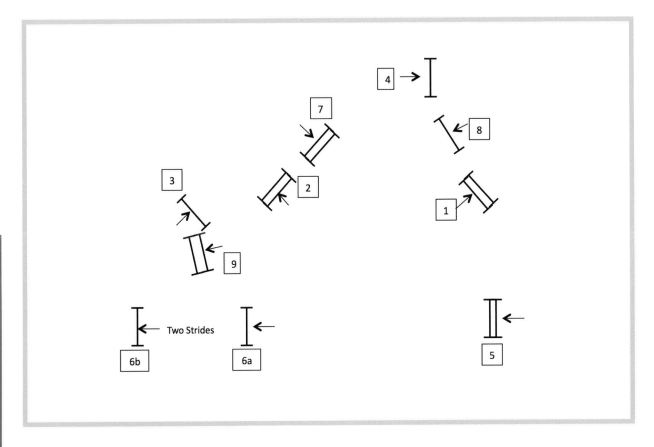

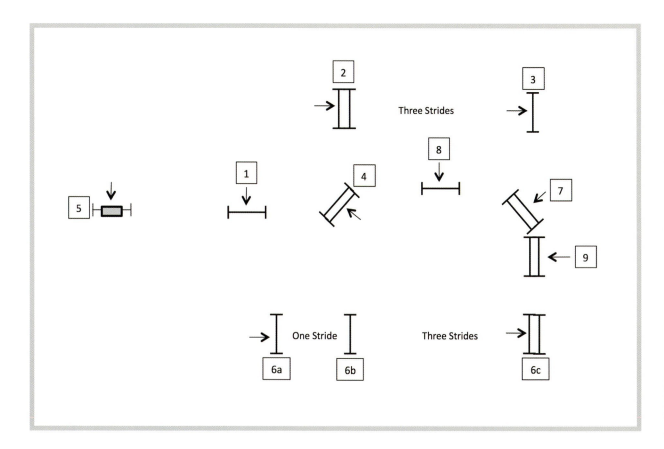

INTERMEDIATE JUMPER COURSE 12

NOTES: Leave plenty of room between the triple combination and the rail (at least 8 feet and preferably 10 to 12 feet) as there are several parts of this track that take you through the middle of the three-stride section (#6b to #6c). Part of the challenge of this course is to reestablish your pace after the Liverpool (Fence #5), as it will tend to make your horse lengthen and the combination that follows is one stride to three strides, which requires engagement and collection in order to execute it without faults.

COURSE COMPOSITION	
11	Total Number of Obstacles
5	Total Number of Verticals
6	Total Number of Oxers
11	Wing Standards (pairs)
6	Schooling Standards (pairs)
11	Filler Items
28	Poles (less if fillers are used)
11	Ground Lines or Flower Boxes
56	Jump Cups

INTERMEDIATE JUMPER COURSE 13

NOTES: This course has two double combinations, one off the right lead and one off the left lead. It also has two bending lines, one off either lead.

COURSE COMPOSITION	
11	Total Number of Obstacles
5	Total Number of Verticals
6	Total Number of Oxers
11	Wing Standards (pairs)
6	Schooling Standards (pairs)
11	Filler Items
28	Poles (less if fillers are used)
11	Ground Lines or Flower Boxes
56	Jump Cups

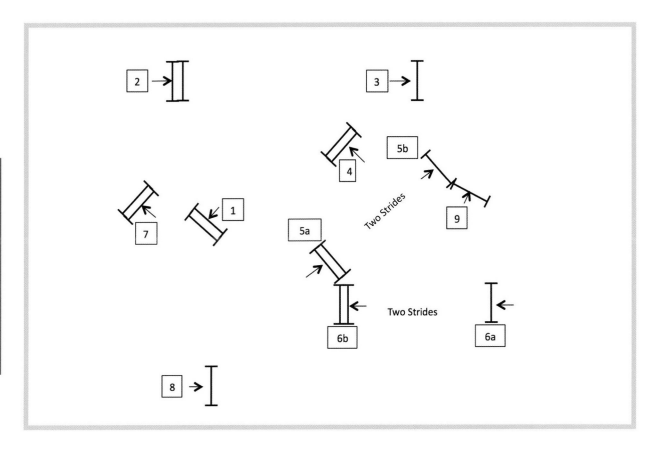

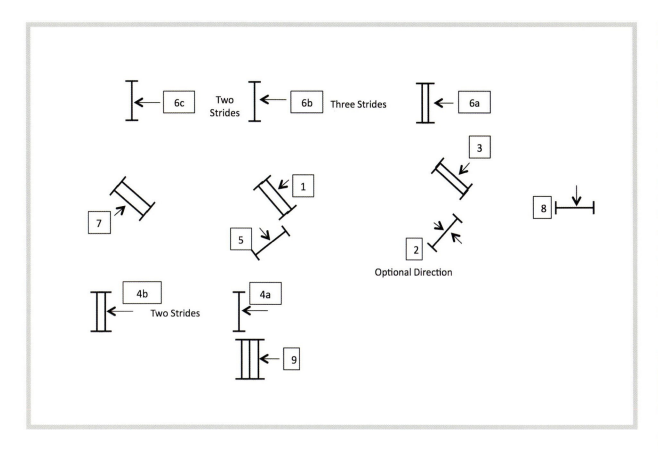

INTERMEDIATE JUMPER COURSE 14

NOTES: Think about how you want the triple combination (#6a/b/c) to ride before you set this course. If you use standard distances, the three-stride oxer to vertical (#6a to #6b) might ride a little long, whereas the two-stride vertical to vertical (#6b to #6c) might ride a little short. Leave room between the triple combination and the rail, at least 8 feet (preferably 10 to 12 feet), and do the same for the end fence (#8). After Fence #1, the rider can choose to turn either right or left. The direction you turn going from Fence #1 to #2 will determine the size of the rollback turn you will take on the approach to #3.

COURSE COMPOSITION	
12	Total Number of Obstacles
6	Total Number of Verticals
6	Total Number of Oxers
12	Wing Standards (pairs)
7	Schooling Standards (pairs)
12	Filler Items
31	Poles (less if fillers are used)
12	Ground Lines or Flower Boxes
62	Jump Cups

INTERMEDIATE JUMPER COURSE 15

NOTES: This course starts with an oxer to oxer line on the diagonal out of a short corner. This means the rider needs to establish a forward pace from the very beginning of the course. It features both a double and a triple combination.

COURSE COMPOSITION	
12	Total Number of Obstacles
6	Total Number of Verticals
6	Total Number of Oxers
12	Wing Standards (pairs)
6	Schooling Standards (pairs)
12	Filler Items
30	Poles (less if fillers are used)
12	Ground Lines or Flower Boxes
60	Jump Cups

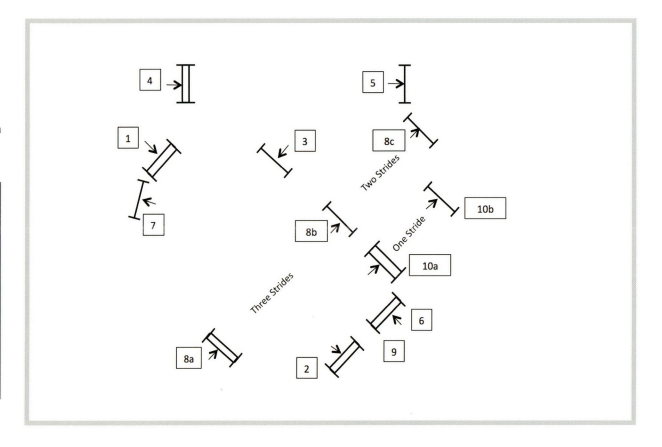

8

Getting What You Need
Materials, Cost, and Upkeep

- **A Brief Introduction to Jump Component Materials**
- **What You Need**
- **Build or Buy?**
- **Managing the Budget**
- **Storage**

A BRIEF INTRODUCTION TO JUMP COMPONENT MATERIALS

If you plan to design and build school courses for practice purposes, you'll need a basic supply of equipment that is in good repair. Your training or boarding facility may already have jump components available to you; or, you may need to consider the best way to build a sufficient inventory with a limited budget.

Jump components are made from wood, PVC (polyvinyl chloride), HDPE (high-density polyethylene), PPL (polypropylene), or a combination of these materials. As a point of reference, the jumps utilized at horse shows are usually made of wood; they

⋀ Plan to invest in good poles, and plenty of them. Poles are your "best friend" when it comes to keeping cost down and courses simple. They are the easiest component to move around, and you can set a completely relevant course made up of just poles. With a course of poles you can practice track and pace, the two most important parts of jumping a "real" course. Cantering poles is much easier on the horse's joints, so you can practice for a longer period of time. Note the jump cups in photo B; the jump cups should be removed from the standards when you are going to be riding between them.

are removed and stored when the event is over so the weather doesn't affect their quality and safety over time.

Wood jumps, which can come in any color or style, are quite heavy and require painting and regular repair (especially when left outside). This can make their use in everyday schooling impractical. PVC jumps are significantly lighter (and therefore easier to move and set on course), but they can crack when a horse hits them hard or if they are handled roughly. They are also usually limited in color to white or grey, although color can be added with tape.

HDPE and PPL jumps are the most durable and come in a wider selection of colors than their PVC equivalents, but they are also the most expensive. Some HDPE gates and boxes are as heavy as their wood counterparts, which makes them durable but also harder to move and configure than the same components made from PVC or PPL material.

I use components made from all four materials, although in general I do not recommend PVC poles, as they can break and/or crack when a horse hits them, and they are just too lightweight for the horse to respect them, which can be problematic when using them for training purposes.

Wood poles really take a beating and often need to be painted every year. I prefer HDPE or PPL "wrapped" wood poles (wood poles encased in a sealed sleeve of HDPE or PPL) as they never need painting and you can just hose them off as necessary. Because these poles have a wood core, they have enough weight to them to ensure the horses respect them. HDPE and PPL poles show wear when left lying in arena footing and show marks when the horse's hooves hit them, but I have found them to be the most durable of the choices available. They are expensive—so to counter this, I use only 10-foot poles and 10-foot filler elements, as they help maximize rideable space in the arena, they are easier to move, and they are more affordable than their 12-foot counterparts.

WHAT YOU NEED

To set most of the courses in this guide, especially should you choose to add all the fill indicated in the inventory lists (see p. 127 for an example), you need a significant number of jump components. To simplify, and if you are just starting out, I've created the following guide for a course that includes a single vertical fence and two lines, with one vertical and one oxer each (a total of five jumps). To this you can gradually add one vertical and one oxer or specialty jump, such as a Liverpool, as funds and/or time allow. Pretty soon you will have a significant number of jump components to work with, and you will be able to build just about any course you can design.

- Start with schooling standards, which you should always purchase in pairs. You need one pair (two standards) for a vertical fence and two pairs (four stan-

dards) for an oxer. The lines I've described consist of one vertical fence and one oxer (as they usually do). Therefore, you need three pairs of standards (six standards) for every line you plan to set. When you have two lines, as in my sample case, you need six pairs (12 standards). A single vertical fence requires an additional pair (two standards), so for this mini-course you need a total of seven pairs of schooling standards (14 individual standards).

- You want a minimum of two but preferably three to four poles per set of standards. This allows you to have at least two poles for a vertical (if you are not using any other fill) and one pole for a ground line. For an oxer with no other fill, you need two poles on the front element and one pole on the back element, with one pole for a ground line. For my sample five-jump mini-course, I recommend 20 poles.

◀ Here is a small, five-jump course, with a five-stride line (vertical to an oxer), two single verticals and a single oxer. This course uses seven pairs of schooling standards (14 total), four homemade plank-type fillers, and 12 poles. This course, as set, does not have any poles for ground lines. You would need five more poles to set a ground line for every jump.

- You need two jump cups for every pole (and also two jump cups for any hanging filler that you may be using).

- You need to choose between hanging fillers (gates or planks) or hurdles/boxes that sit on the ground under a pole, between the standards. I recommend getting hanging fillers that are about 12 to 18 inches in height, as you can easily raise them by adjusting the cups that the filler rests in. I also suggest buying filler in "pairs" so that when you construct a line or combination, the obstacles in the line or combination can be made similar. For the purposes of our sample mini-course, you need five filler elements and ten cups when the fillers will hang from the standards.

QUICK REFERENCE
For a mini-course of five jumps with one single vertical fence and two lines, each consisting of a vertical and an oxer (a total of three verticals and two oxers), you need:

- Seven pairs of schooling standards (14 individual standards)

- 20 poles (when no other filler is used)

- Five filler elements (optional)

- Approximately 24 to 50 jump cups, depending on how you build your fences.

Note: A typical course at a horse show is a minimum of seven jumps. For a starter course I would recommend adding an additional vertical and an additional oxer. This adds three more sets of standards, bringing the total to 10 pairs (20 individual standards), plus an additional 12 poles (total of 32), two additional fillers (total of seven), and 10 more jump cups.

BUILD OR BUY?

When you have basic carpentry skills and the right tools, building jumps yourself instead of purchasing ready-made jump components may save you money. However, *you must use common sense* as safety of horse and rider is of primary importance. There are a number of books available that include plans for building jumps, and you can find instructions for jump construction on the Internet, but those you choose to follow should be in accordance with safety standards.

I have seen a number of plans for building jumps available on the Internet that I found just plain horrifying—while course design allows for creativity, actual jump material should never be flimsy or dangerous. Making a jump out of a stack of cement blocks, using lawn chairs as standards, or attaching permanent hooks to standards instead of jump cups is *never* a good idea! I have also seen frequent recommendations for using PVC pipe from home improvement stores (meant for plumb-

∧ This is an example of hurdles (the fill below the pole) made from PVC material, with green tape added for color. They illustrate a very simple construction, which could easily be made using 2- by 4-inch lumber. However, I recommend that you cost compare before buying lumber and building yourself, as PVC hurdles such as these may be less expensive than building them from wood. These hurdles, from JumPVC, are 2 feet high and 3 feet wide and are shipped unassembled (www.jumpvc.com).

ing) for jump poles. As I've mentioned, I do not use PVC poles as a rule because they are too lightweight and they crack and break easily.

So, when you plan to build your own jumps, make sure that they are safe and sturdy, keeping these four rules of thumb in mind:

- You want the components to be heavy enough for the horse to respect them.

- When a horse hits the jump or steps on the components, you want them to be strong enough to withstand the impact.

> The base on a wing standard, which supports slats, panels, or planks between two posts, should use 2- by 8-inch treated lumber. You need two, 3-foot base pieces for each wing standard. As with schooling standards, the ends should be angle-cut and the base secured to the post(s) with carriage bolts.

∧ Build the base of a schooling standard to support a single 4- by 4-inch post. Four 18-inch pieces of 2- by 6-inch treated lumber, with the ends angled for safety, works well. Secure the base pieces to the post with carriage bolts (*do not* use screws, as shown here).

In A you see a metal jump cup with a chain welded to the pin so the pin will not be lost in the footing, and in B a plastic variation with rope attached to the pin. Plastic jump cups can be turned over so that they are flat if needed (see bottom cup). Note: When using jump cups that attach to standards with pins, be sure that the pin goes all the way through the cup and the post of the standard and is through the hole on the jump cup on the other side.

Photo C shows an FEI-approved safety cup from Hi-Tech Horse Jumps (www.hitechhorsejumps.com). It is attached to the standards via two hooks and will fall with a pole or fill element if hit. These cups can also be turned over so they are flat.

In D you see an example of a keyhole track and pinless safety cups. Notice the cup holding the gate has been turned upside down so it is flat. You can buy adapters for keyhole-type cups so they meet FEI safety cup requirements.

> When building your own jumps, using keyhole tracks that simply screw into your standard posts is the easiest way to attach jump cups. In photo A you can clearly see the 48-inch tracks I used on these homemade standards (keyhole tracks come in a variety of lengths). The bottom of the track is about 12 inches from the ground, as shown in B. Note that I used bolts to attach the bases to the posts for stability. I put tracks on both sides of these standards so I could use them to make an option fence like the one in C. Photo D offers a close-up of the ground line on the post-and-rail option: I used old fence posts with floral foam tucked in the holes to secure artificial flowers, creating an attractive "flower box."

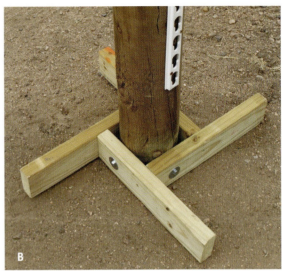

GETTING WHAT
YOU NEED

- Components are frequently dragged around the arena, rather than carried, so joints of standards and fill need to be secure so they don't pull apart.

- Components are constantly exposed to the weather and gritty abrasive sand, so they need to stand up to wear and tear from the elements.

Building jumps is not complex, but you do need to have a circular saw and electric drill with a hole saw/auger bit. A drill press is even better, as you need to be able to drill holes for jump cups straight through your standards. Another option is to use *keyhole tracks* with safety cups. Keyhole tracks are fairly cheap and easy to install—they simply screw onto the post of the jump standard, eliminating the need to drill holes. With keyhole tracks you know that the holes for fence height adjustment are in the correct place and that the jump cups will fit your standards. However, before you go too far be aware that the pinless safety cups that you have to use with keyhole tracks *are* expensive. They are usually sold individually, as opposed to jump cups with pins that are sold in pairs for about the same price as a single pinless safety cup.

The biggest drawback to making your own jumps (in my opinion) is the painting that is required. Each piece of every component should be sanded, caulked, primed, and painted (and probably touched up every year), or

they won't last and they will look terrible. Wood requires maintenance—it's that simple. On the other hand, if you like to paint or if there are young riders at the barn who would enjoy the opportunity to be creative, this aspect of jump component creation and maintenance can be fun and a source of community-building.

TIPS FOR CONSTRUCTING JUMPS

- Jump components should be constructed with 4- by 4-inch lumber for posts, 2- by 4-inch lumber for frames, and 5/8-inch outdoor quality plywood for panels and facing material.

- Use bolts and/or screws (*not* nails) to attach the pieces.

- Any part of a jump component that comes into contact with the ground should be made of pressure-treated lumber.

- Materials for most components, such as standards, gates, and planks, can be purchased at your local lumber store. However, it is hard to find jump poles in a 3½- to 4-inch diameter at a 10- to 12-foot length at a lumber store. You may be able to find 8-foot lengths, which can work if you make your own filler elements to match. Note that filler items from ready-made jump suppliers typically come in 10- to 12-foot widths. A compromise may be to purchase unfinished poles

from a jump supplier (see p. 209 for a list of recommendations) and paint them yourself.

- You will need to purchase jump cups and/or keyhole tracks for your standards (even if you build the standards yourself). Most jump suppliers and some tack stores sell these parts.

MANAGING THE BUDGET

As I stated early in this chapter, safety for horse and rider should be your primary concern when buying or building jumps. When cost is your next most important issue, go with fewer jumps and build your inventory slowly. The easiest way to keep the cost down at first is to use only poles and simple schooling standards, deferring purchase of filler elements and wings.

And as I said before, there is no reason you can't begin with jump courses furnished with just poles. You can create and use every course in this book with just poles (12 to 16 poles should be sufficient). Cantering over a course of ground poles is technically difficult for the rider because of the accuracy required for establishing pace and guiding the horse on the proper track, and since the horse thinks he is just "cantering around," he won't help the rider as much by sighting in on the "jumps." When you can canter a course of poles without any misses, you will be amazed how well you can ride an actual course of jumps.

> Here are three examples of a basic "wall" that can be easily constructed rather than purchased ready-made. All three are 2 feet high, 12 inches deep, and 5 feet, 11 inches wide, built on a 2- by 4-inch frame and faced with 5/8-inch plywood. They are extremely heavy and take two people to lift and/or move them. These particular walls were made to sit two at a time in a 12-foot wide jump, and they also work great individually as a filler for "skinny" jumps. The wall on the left is covered with artificial turf, the middle wall is painted in a brick pattern, and the white wall on the right is faced with board and batten and then painted.

When beginning to build a jump inventory, simple components, such as the poles and planks shown in A are a great way to start out. These types of components allow the most versatility in terms of height adjustment, and are easy lift and move (the plank is from Burlingham Sports and the poles are from Hi-Tech Horse Jumps).

There are two important things to note when using just poles on the ground for your jump course: make sure the poles are heavy and sturdy enough that they won't roll or break if a horse steps or trips over them, and only use one pole for each "jump," even when the course diagram calls for an oxer, triple bar, or Liverpool (for example). With poles on the ground, you are practicing pace and track, not jumping style over width and height.

Riders at my farm have a lot of different kinds of jump components available to them, and yet it seems that their trainers use poles and cross-rails for about 90 percent of their work. Never underestimate the value of the simplicity of poles.

OTHER WAYS TO KEEP THE COST DOWN

When your budget can handle more components there

> The line in photo A is typical of what you will see in the hunter ring at a horse show, with a vertical as the first fence and an oxer as the second fence, and fill that is representative of the fence construction used for the hunters. The line in photo B is more like what you'd see in a jumper class, with an oxer as the first fence, little fill, and no ground lines. Note that the small picket gate is used as part of both the hunter-type and the jumper-type fences. Small picket gates like these are extremely useful because of their versatility, and they are less expensive and easier to move than larger fill components.

A

B

are several ways to keep the cost of acquiring them within reason.

• Purchase, or build, schooling standards, rather than wing standards, as they are significantly less expensive (whether you are building or buying them) and they conserve space in your arena. They are also lighter and easier to move around.

• Buy, or build, filler elements that are shorter in height, preferably in the 12- to 18-inch height range. The cost for shorter filler elements is less, and frankly, they are more versatile, as you can raise hanging filler elements or add additional poles over the top of a filler element when you need more height. Because of the lower height, you can still use them for horses and riders at a variety of experience levels.

• When you like to build things (but perhaps don't enjoy painting), disassembled PVC and PVC/wood combination kits for standards and fill are available for purchase. They generally have a lower price point than jumps that are assembled and shipping is less as the items are packaged so they lie flat.

- When you like to paint, but you don't have carpentry skills or the tools necessary to make everything from scratch, you can buy fully prepared wooden kits that you simply bolt together and paint as you desire. (A big bonus is that standards come with the jump cup holes properly spaced and drilled.) Unfinished wooden kits and preparing/building the components from scratch are probably the most economical ways to go when building a jump inventory. I suggest you price shop before choosing one over the other.

- Before you build or buy jump components, check out the jump vendors that have rental (usually by the month) or "lease-to-own" programs. Depending on your schooling program and inventory needs, they may provide a reasonable way to supplement your stock of components from time to time. And, sometimes rental vendors have components that can be purchased at a discount.

- Finally, keep an eye out for "used" jumps. Jumps can come up for sale online at any time, and good deals can be found. At the end of the season, many show management companies sell their jumps, and you can get an entire course for a much reduced price (although that doesn't necessarily mean cheap!). Also, note that elements from a show course are likely 12 feet in width, so may not work in smaller arenas. Be prepared to make repairs on used jumps.

STORAGE

Jump components need to be properly stored so you can get to them easily and so they can be protected from wear and tear. When jump components are left out in the arena, even when not in use, they take up rideable space and no matter what they are made of, they will deteriorate when left exposed to the elements. Unused jump components left lying in a ring—especially poles and jump cups—not only warp, rot, and rust, they are a safety hazard.

Because of their size, shape, and weight, jump components are actually not easy to store. At the very least,

◀ Storage for jump components doesn't have to be fancy, but it should be neat and organized. Properly storing and maintaining components goes a long way in extending their life.

you need a shed or covered space that is clean and dry, and of a large enough size that your tallest standards and longest poles can be accommodated. Wings and schooling standards should be grouped for storage by type and color, since you will want a pair of matching standards for each jump you set. It also makes it easier when other matching jump components are stored nearby.

A *pole caddy*, which is a specialized cart configured to hold poles and gates, is a great addition when possible. The one at my farm has enough room on its flatbed to hold flower boxes. A caddy allows you to store your poles off the ground, and makes it easy to move them indoors and outdoors as necessary.

It always helps add to jump component longevity to take a few minutes and hose different elements of your course off before putting them away.

> I really like to use a pole caddy, such as this one from www.getjumps.com.

About the Author

Originally from Columbus, Ohio, Susan D. Tinder showed Quarter Horses in her early years, and in 1982 she was named the Ohio Quarter Horse Association's Reserve All-Around Amateur. Sue was high point in Western horsemanship, English equitation, and hunter under saddle. She also accumulated points in hunter hack, amateur trail, and amateur pole bending on her horse Lady Biddersweet, as well as numerous other all-around awards across the state of Ohio.

Sue then went on to a 25-year career in accounting and finance, holding such positions as Treasurer for LCI International, Inc., Managing Director for McLernon and Associates, Ltd., Controller for the Rummler-Brache Group, Ltd., and Executive Vice President for Dynegy, Inc.

Following the sale of a telecom broadband company that she helped found, Sue retired from corporate life and made her way back into the horse world. For the last 15 years she has shown a number of horses on the "AA" rated hunter/jumper circuit and has been successful on both coasts.

Sue purchased her farm, Tolland Falls, in 2003. Sue continues to manage the farm's evolution into one of Colorado's most respected equestrian facilities. Under the guidance of Micca and Randy Henry (Winsome Farms, Castle Rock, Colorado), Sue currently shows her horses, Five Nines and Braxton, in the Adult Amateur Hunter Division.

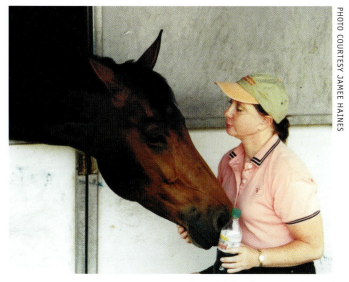

PHOTO COURTESY JAMEE HAINES

Sue with her horse Marcus at a show in Albuquerque, New Mexico.

	WHERE TO BUY — VENDORS	
Vendor Name	**Website**	**Comments**
JUMP SUPPLIERS		
Burlingham Sports	www.burlinghamsports.com	Manufacturer of HDPE Products including jump components, poles, dressage arenas, and stable equipment. Does not sell retail. To purchase you must go through a distributor.
Hi-Tech Horse Jumps the US distributor for JUMP4JOY	www.hitechhorsejumps.com	British manufacturer of PPL jumps and poles. Website is for the US distributor. Geared toward the jumper ring and event riders. One of a few manufacturers who manufacture eventing type jumps. Also will rent jumps for horse shows and offers a lease-own program.
Premier Equestrian	www.dressagearena.net	Sells their own line of PVC jumps, poles, and dressage arenas called "PolyPro." Also a distributor for Burlingham products. They sell arena footing and arena related products.
Jumps West	www.jumpswest.com	Sells their own line of PVC/wood combination jumps and poles as well as special order wood jumps. Also a distributor for Burlingham products. They sell arena footing and arena-related products.
Jump PVC	www.jumpvc.com	Sells their own line of PVC jump components. Usually shipped unassembled.
Next Day Jumps	www.nextdayjumps.com	Sells their own line of combination wood and PVC jumps. Shipped unassembled. Some are shipped unpainted.
Jumps USA	www.jumpsusa.com	PVC jump components and dressage arenas. Shipped unassembled.
CCI Quality Horse Show Jumps	www.getjumps.com	New and used show quality wood jumps. Also sells arena equipment including pole caddies.
STORAGE EQUIPMENT AND POLE CADDIES		
CCI Quality Horse Show Jumps	www.getjumps.com	New and used pole racks and caddies.
COURSE DESIGN RESOURCES		
Eduard Petrovic	www.jumpdesign.net	Many examples of jump courses that can be printed from the web. Also free PowerPoint course design templates that can be downloaded to your computer.
Medal and Maclay Courses	www.medalmaclay.com	Reprints of equitation courses from the ASPCA Maclay and other Medal Classes from 1984 to 2005.

(continued on p. 210)

Where to Buy — Vendors (continued)

Vendor Name	Website	Comments
ARENA EQUIPMENT		
ABI Equine	www.abiequine.com	Distributor of arena grooming products; multiple manufacturers, including Kiser.
FICS of Maryland, Inc.	www.stableandarena.com	Distributor of arena grooming products; multiple manufacturers, including Red Master. Also sells footing products.
Parma Company, Inc.	www.parmacompany.com	Manufacturer of Parma Arena Groomers.
D.J. Reveal	www.reveal4-n-1.com	Manufacturer and distributor of Reveal Arena Drags.
West Coast Footings	www.westcoastfootings.com	Distributor of arena grooming products, multiple manufacturers including Red Master. Also sells footing products.
DECORATIONS		
Silk Tree Warehouse	www.silktreewarehouse.com	Sells wholesale trees and shrubs.
Improvements	www.ImprovementsCatalog.com	Sells artificial rocks and other decorative items.
Dollar Tree	www.dollartree.com	Cheap silk flowers in bulk. Selection is varied.
Dollar Store	www.dollarstore.com	Cheap silk flowers in bulk. Selection is varied and sometimes limited.
Flower Factory Super Store	www.flowerfactory.com	Sells wholesale silk flowers.
PLANS FOR BUILDING HORSE JUMPS		
Equi Jump Plans and Products	http://equijumpplans.tripod.com	20 plans for building jump standards and fill elements.

BOOKS WITH INSTRUCTIONS FOR BUILDING JUMPS

Author Name	Publisher	Title
Campbell, Lisa	Half Halt Press, Inc.: 2000	*Jumps, etc.: Jumps, Dressage Arenas and Stable Equipment You Can Build*
Radford, Andy	Crowood Press: 2005	*Building Show Jumps*
Gordon-Watson, Mary	Half Halt Press, Inc.: 1988	*Making Your Own Show Jumps*

Bibliography

Allen, Linda, *101 Jumping Exercises for Horse & Rider*. North Adams, Massachusetts: Storey Publishing, 2002.

Blingnault, Karin. *Equine Biomechanics for Riders: The Key to Balanced Riding.* London: J.A. Allen, 2009.

Coldrey, Christopher. *Courses for Horses: A Complete Guide to Designing and Building Show Jumping Courses.* London: J.A. Allen, 1978.

De Némethy, Bertalan. *The De Némethy Method: Modern Techniques for Training the Show Jumper and Its Rider.* New York, New York: Doubleday, 1988.

Dillon, Ernest and Revington, Helen. *Show Jumping for Fun or Glory: A Training Manual for Successful Show Jumping at All Levels*. London: Kenilworth Press Ltd., 2000.

Gego, Arno. *Course Design: Historical Roots, Theory, Practice, Aesthetics, Ethics and State of the Art.* London: J.A. Allen, 2006.

Kursinski, Anne. *Anne Kursinski's Riding and Jumping Clinic: A Step by Step Course for Winning in the Hunter and Jumper Rings*. North Pomfret, Vermont: Trafalgar Square Books, 2011.

Morris, George H. *Hunter Seat Equitation. Third Edition.* New York: Doubleday, 1990.

Savoie, Jane. *Dressage 101: The Ultimate Source of Dressage Basics in a Language You Can Understand.* North Pomfret, Vermont: Trafalgar Square Books, 2011.

Summers, Maureen. *Basic Course Building.* Wykey, Shrewsbury: Kenilworth Press, Ltd, 1991.

Teall, Geoff. *Geoff Teall on Riding Hunters, Jumpers and Equitation: Develop a Winning Style.* North Pomfret, Vermont: Trafalgar Square Books, 2006.

United State Dressage Federation. *Under Foot: The United States Dressage Federation Guide to Arena Construction, Maintenance and Repair.* Lexington, Kentucky: USDF, 2007.

United States Hunter Jumper Association. *The USHJA Trainer Certification Program Manual.* Lexington, Kentucky: USHJA, 2007.

White-Mullin, Anna Jane. *The Complete Guide to Hunter Seat Training, Showing, and Judging.* North Pomfret, Vermont: Trafalgar Square Books, 2008.

ADDITIONAL READING on the training of horses and riders in the jumping disciplines can be found by visiting the United States Hunter Jumper Association's website: www.ushja.org. I recommend reviewing the list of suggested reading material for the Trainer Certification Program (select the "Visit the TCP Bookstore" link).

Index

Adult Amateur Hunter fence heights/ classes, 120

Amateur Owner Working Hunter fence heights/classes, 120

Angled tracks, 15–16

Arena footing

    fence types and, 10–14

    and horse's perspective of structural elements, 7–10

    and jump anatomy, 5–7. *See also* Jumps

    jump course terminology, 14–19

    type/management of, 2–5

Arenas (small). *See* Small arenas

Arrowhead, 13

Ascending oxers, 10–11, 27-30

Baby Green Hunter fence heights/ classes, 120

Bascule, 22–23, 26–27, 29

Base of arenas, 2–3

Beginner classes, direction changes and, 16–17

Bending/broken line exercises, 80

Blind spots of horses, 7–8

Bonding agents for footing, 5

Budgets, 202–205

Building a course. *See* Course setting/ building; Materials/cost/upkeep

Cavalletti, 13–14. *See also* Grids/ gymnastics/mini-courses

Change of direction, 14

Children Hunter Pony fence heights/ classes, 120

Children Hunters fence heights/classes, 120

Circular tracks, 15

Color in jumps

    horse discrimination of, 8

    jump course drawings and, 53–57

    in space-saving configurations, 91

    visibility and, 62–63

    Combinations

    advanced/medal equitation courses and, 145

    definitions of, 16, 18

    differences between one-stride, 26

    jumper courses and, 188–192

    one-stride, 134

    takeoff/landing distances for, 28, 30

Conformation Hunter fence heights/ classes, 120

Coop, 144

Corner fences, 13

Costs. *See* Materials/cost/upkeep

Course design theory

    art of, 33–34

    circles/turns/angles and, 44–48

    cross-measuring and, 40, 42–44

    geometry of, 34–35

    and levels of difficulty, 36–38

    placing first fence, 39–41

    quick reference considerations, 49–50

    schooling vs. showing courses, 31–33

    track design, 38–40

Course designers, licensed, 1

Course diagram, 59

Course setting/building

    decorating, 64–66

    how to, 59–62

FIVE NINES (aka "Rueben")
Indio, California
36" x 48" Original Oil Painting
by Sharon Lynn Campbell – 2009